and so, I write ...

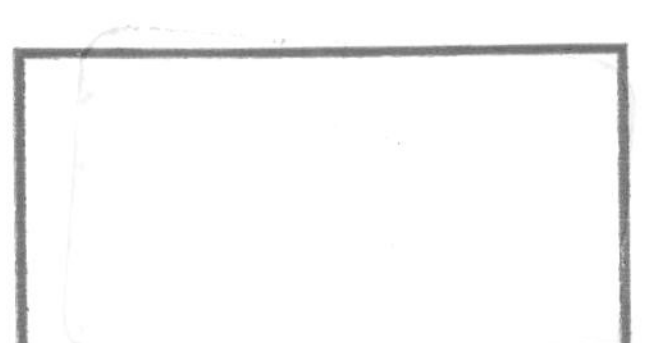

A collection of plays, programs, meditations, poems and more

Written by

Omega Flowers

Mantel Publishing
P. O. Box 361281
Decatur, Georgia 30034

AND SO, I WRITE ...

A Collection of Plays, Programs, Meditations
And Poems
Written by Omega Flowers

Edited by Sabrina Flowers Rogers

REPRODUCIBLE

Copies of the plays and programs may be made if:

1. You are the original purchaser
2. You are using the copies for non-commercial purposes (such as teaching and other church ministries)
3. You use the instructions provided with the plays and programs.

e-mail: flores999@aol.com
P.O. Box 361281
Decatur, Georgia 30034

All scripture quotations and references are taken from the Holy Bible; the Quest Study Bible, International Version, copyright 1984 by Zondervan Corporation; and the King James Version Study Bible, copyright 2002 by Zondervan Corporation. **Other Resources:** The New National Baptist Hymnal, National Baptist Publishing Board, copyright 1977; portions of songs (lyrics only) are used. Bible Readings for the Home, Review and Herald Publishing Association, copyright 1950. *(Copyright owner not found).* Encyclopedia of the Bible, Baker Book House, copyright 1988. *(Permission granted)*

PUBLISHER: Mantel Publishing
P.O. Box 361281
Decatur, Georgia 30034

Printed in the United States of America
Library of Congress
ISBN: 0-2761600-1-5

Front cover designed by James Johnson, Associate Illustrator
Back Cover by Sabrina Flowers Rogers

CONTENTS

DEDICATION

This book is dedicated prayerfully to the memory of my mother who believed in working with children, inspiring them to do their very best in the sight of God. She taught them how to learn poems and speeches, say them with expression and feelings, and to rejoice in their effort and successes.

To the memory of my father whose love, strength, and dedication to the work of the church caused him to stand head and shoulders above many men. For many years he organized and directed the Sunday School Department of the church.

To the memory of Simonetta Z. Smith whose faith seemed as solid as a rock, and whose dedication to the Sunday School and the Charles G. Adams Drama Group was unwavering. Her wisdom, concerns and nurture for young children inspired me to try to walk in her footsteps.

To my children whose faith in me and my dedication to teaching kept me praising God for many blessings. My inspiration was fueled by their insistence that next to them, other children needed what I had to offer in the name of Jesus, and they did it unselfishly.

To my church and Pastor, Dr. Charles Gilchrist Adams, who gave me the great opportunity to continue the work of the Drama Group and other work with the youth in the church. His leadership has been a blessed presence in my life.

And to Cora, my friend and co-worker, Thanks!

Thank you, Sabrina, for insisting that, *"I Write"*

ABOUT THE AUTHOR

Omega Flowers now lives in Atlanta, Georgia. She was born in Tennessee; the seventh child of ten children. She was educated there with the exception of graduate studies in Michigan.

Omega began writing as a teacher in the Detroit Public School system. Very early in her teaching career, she realized a greater need to work closer with teens in assisting with development and problem solving. She became a Guidance Counselor, and later a Guidance Administrator. Working with children in the church was an extra rewarding experience.

Now retired, she joined the Greenforest Community Baptist Church in Decatur, Georgia, pastored by Dr. George O. McCalep, Jr. She spends time working with children in the "Be Smart Kids" program. This program supplements basic skills training and readiness through exercises on the computer. In addition to other church ministries, she still finds time to read and to write.

Omega has two children, Kevin and Sabrina, and four grandchildren; Kevin, Jr., Justine, and Benjamin Flowers, and Alexis Rogers.

ACKNOWLEDGMENTS

My writing has spanned over many years. At least two of the poems were written while I was a high school student. However, when I began working with children in the public school system and in church, I became anxious about extracurricular teaching and guiding youth in positive experiences. This was the beginning of writing the plays and programs.

I have been encouraged by my family and many friends, especially in the church. For 25 years, my pastor, Dr. Charles Adams of the Hartford Church has inspired and counseled me in many of my efforts. I also owe a great debt of gratitude to my friend Gayle McCarter. We worked together side by side with the youth of the church in Youth Council, planning retreats, and other activities. Also, Cora Pearson, who has a great flair for the dramatics, was co-sponsor and co-director for many of the productions and activities. Her creativity has been an inspiration to me in many of my endeavors. The Superintendent of the Sunday School, Curtis Kilpatrick, has been a 'right arm' over the years. And I must give credit to the constant core of our audience for most of our activities. The Mother's Board of the church could be counted on for attendance, promotions, and blessings.

I cannot begin to list all the sources of inspiration, but the greatest of them all are the children. They will forever be a part of the spirit that keeps me loving them and assisting wherever I can. I am concerned about the growth and welfare of all young people.

Associate Illustrator, James Doyle Johnson, Jr. could not be replaced by anyone greater for this work. I keep him close because of the family relationship and his artistic ability.

And to all I have not mentioned, Thank You!

Omega Flowers

PREFACE – NOTES TO THE READER

And So, I Write is primarily a collection of plays and programs written while I was a member of Hartford Memorial Baptist Church in Detroit, Michigan. They were written for presentation by children in the Sunday School and the Charles G. Adams Drama Group. As a worker with the youth organizations, my motivation was to facilitate Christian maturity through many activities that would encourage and deepen worship, and the study of God's word.

Drama is an exciting method of helping children with Christian values. In our society today where so many unsavory activities and negative attitudes are prevalent, drama and especially programs that depict good moral values are great teaching tools for building self-esteem. Children benefit from feeling they are a part of something positive.

Plays in this work center around many of the familiar Bible accounts which young people in the church have already read and are somewhat familiar with. They help them visualize how God works with His people. In getting involved, the children experience a number of learning processes such as:

1. Learning scripture and experiencing the love of God
2. Developing a deeper appreciation for the Word of God
3. Learning stage presentation
4. Improving upon speech deliverance
5. Further developing memorization skills
6. Building self-esteem
7. Improving relationships in groups

Some of the subject matter is presented to assist young people with many concerns they are faced with today. Many times they may not know how to respond to adversity, or to handle situations they face on a daily basis.

Most of the programs in this book were written to commemorate special occasions. The Sunday School is a perfect place to develop appreciation for one's place in life and his or her heritage. The drama ministry at Hartford Church was well embraced by the congregation and the pastor.

Although many of the plays and programs are lengthy, it was a refreshing experience to teach young people to memorize lines. Reading was an important part of this process. This is why it was necessary to read the Bible stories and other related materials, discuss them, and make the characters become a part of the participants. Rehearsals become delightful experiences.

You will note that some of the plays have elaborate sets and scenery. It is most important that the young people are involved in both the development and construction. You will find unusual talent and enthusiasm.

Other selections, reports and articles are products of study groups, classes and personal research. The poems and miscellaneous selections are meditations and pleasant moments.

It is my prayer that you will find the activities and articles in this book as delightful and enjoyable as I found in writing them.

One

and

Two Act

Plays

The Greatest Gift Of All 8

For God so loved the world, that He gave his only begotten Son, that whosoever believeth in Him should not perish, but have everlasting life.

John 3:16

The Greatest Gift Of All

CHARACTERS

Three teens try to cheer up a friend

Robin

Mary Mike

Sandra

Robin's Mother

Mrs. Brown, a neighbor

Mitzi, Mrs. Brown's daughter

Other teens join for singing carols

THE GREATEST GIFT OF ALL

SCENE 1

Robin is home alone in more ways than one. It's the Christmas season, school is out, and there is nothing to do. She is seated in her living room going through a magazine, scarcely seeing the pages. There is a pattern of getting up, walking to the window, returning and slumping down on the couch again.

Robin: Gosh! I'm so bored I could scream! *(She hurls the magazine across the room)* I can't stand this, this Christmas stuff. Everybody's grinning and just trying to be so happy. What's that all about?

(She drops on the couch again) If only I had waited for Marsha, Brad and the rest coming home from school. I was sure during fifth period Brad wanted to talk with me; probably would have asked to see me during the holidays. *(She walks around the room with her arms outstretched)* But that gabby little Susan. She just wouldn't leave him alone. I could just kill her! Or, maybe I should 'cash out' myself. Nobody would miss me. Not even my mother. And where is she today? Gone to a luncheon with her friends; that's nothing new. And this is my first vacation day. Some vacation!

(She paces around the room) I wonder if Dad were here would he care? What am I talking about? He didn't even say goodbye to me when he stormed out the door! I guess he was sick of my socialite Mom. But what about me?

(From the window she could see Sandra coming to her house) Oh, no! Not Sandra. I don't need any company now. I don't want to see anybody!

(Sandra knocks. Robin opens the door)

Sandra: Hi, Robin! What are you doing today?

Robin: Nothing. Just enjoying my boring house.

Sandra: Is your mom home?

Robin: No. She had a luncheon today. And after that, I'm sure she will be running around downtown shopping.

Sandra: Are you going down to meet her?

Robin: Fat chance! But I didn't want to go out anyway. I don't enjoy shopping.

Sandra: Then why don't you come to my house with me. I have some gifts to wrap for the little children down the street. You know, the Jensen family. You can help me!

Robin: Yuk! That doesn't sound like a lot of fun to me. And why are you giving them gifts? They have two parents.

Sandra: Yes, but there are so many of them. And remember their house caught fire about three months ago. I understand most of the children's clothing and things in their room were destroyed. They are struggling.

Robin: What kind of gifts are you giving?

Sandra: I have four dolls – my dolls, and I have made new dresses for all of them. I am giving them to the girls. And for the boys, my dad bought ... Oh, come on and I'll show you.

Robin: Okay! Let me leave a note – not that she will ... she probably won't be back anytime soon anyway. *(She writes the note and they start toward the door)*

Girl, you must be nuts. I don't give my things to anyone. I packed all my dolls in a box upstairs. Maybe I will have some children of my own some day.

Sandra: But some child could be playing with them this year. Maybe children won't like playing with dolls by the time you get married and have a family.

Robin: Huh! Maybe you're right. I'm sure not getting off to a bombshell start where men are concerned. Let's go, before I decide to stay here and work on a plan ...

Sandra: What plan?

(Someone knocks on the door)

Robin: Well, the house of the doomed has suddenly come alive! Who could this be? *(She opens the door)*

Mary and Mike! What brings you to my humble abode?

Mary: My mom said she saw Sandra coming to your house. I was going to visit her, so here we all are. I picked up this straggler along the way.

Mike: Hey, I'm no straggler. You girls should feel like queens to have the "King" to grace your presence!

Robin: Well, come on in. And you too, King Mike. Somehow that doesn't sound kingly. But what the heck!

Sandra: What's up, you guys?

Mary: Well, I thought I would stop by your place a little early and help you finish up your gift wrapping. By that time we could meet the others at the corner and pull the caroling together.

Sandra: Good! Let's just go to my house. I do have a few more to wrap. Robin has agreed to go with me.

Robin: No! You have a lot of help, now. You all go. I'm really not into all this gift wrapping and giving stuff!

Mary: But, Robin! This is the Christmas season. This is the best time of the whole year!

Mike: Yeah! And I can't wait for Santa to come. My dad just might be giving me the 'transpo' machine!

Mary: Yeah, right! Mike you just turned 16. A car? You're kidding, of course.

Mike: Who knows? My dad is full of surprises!

Robin: You guys go on. I'm going to stick around until my mom comes home.

Sandra: But you will meet us for caroling, won't you?

Robin: You guys like to do all that dumb stuff. It's cold outside. Besides, all that singing gets on my nerves.

Mary: Oh, come on, Robin. Singing is fun, and people enjoy it, especially those two ladies on Central Avenue. They always invite us in for hot chocolate.

Mike: Okay, Robin. Maybe you could go down to my house with me. I need some help finishing up the old bike in the garage. I'm going to give it to Tony for Christmas. He's never had a bike

Robin: Holy Joe! Every time I see somebody, they are busy giving some things, and all that Christmas junk! All I hear is "giving, giving, giving". Can't somebody talk about "getting, getting, getting"?

Mike: But, Robin! The Bible says it is more blessed to give than to receive. Anyway, Tony's dad is laid off. He has promised to give Tony a new bike for his birthday. But that's not until September next year.

Robin: Blessed, huh! Why should I give when no one bothers to give me anything?

Sandra: But, Robin ...

Robin: I wanted a new bike two years ago, and I still don't have one. I asked for a camera last year ... only $290.00, but did I get it?

Sandra: Robin, do you remember I offered to give you my bike as soon as I got the new one. That bike was new. My legs were just too long.

Mary: Yes, and remember the camera our math teacher offered to you when he found out you were interested in photography? He only gave it to me because you said you didn't want a used one.

Robin: I know. But I wanted the new one I saw at Meyers.

Mike: You see, Robin, you said nobody ever gives you anything. Maybe you just don't want people to give you gifts. Would you rather us give you money ... like $290.00?

Sandra: Okay, that's enough! Let's lay off Robin now, and go and get ready for caroling. I can wrap the gifts tomorrow. Robin, you have already written the note ..

(Robin's mother comes in)

Mother: Hello, hello! Robin, I'm glad your friends came to keep you company. I really hadn't planned to stay so long.

Robin: Okay, okay. I'm going caroling with them! *(Her frustration is showing. She storms out ahead of the others. They follow)*

SCENE 2

Six to eight carolers in front of the Brown's door singing. Mrs. Brown and her daughter come out to listen. Suggestions: Here We Come A-Caroling; White Christmas; Away in a Manger, etc.

(The family applauds)

Mrs. Brown: Come in, come in! I have some hot chocolate and cookies for you. You must be cold.

Mary: Thank you, Mrs. Brown, but we should be moving along. We got off to a late start.

Mike: But, maybe we have time for a few cookies!

Mary: Mike!

Mrs. Brown: Why, of course. Mitzi, get the box of cookies from the table. You children don't know how much I look forward to this each year. I count this as one of my best gifts.

Sandra: We do love doing this. It makes Christmas all warm and fuzzy!

Mrs. Brown: That's because God has His arms around all of you. This is the kind of gift He wants us to share.

Robin: But why do you call it a gift?

Mrs. Brown: You see, the sharing of ourselves and our talents with others means more to God than all the material gifts we get at Christmastime. Singing about this season and the reason for the season is praising God for his Great Gift to us.

Robin: Well, where is this great ...

Mrs. Brown: You see, God gave us His Son, the Lord Jesus Christ, who blessed us by teaching us how to live in God's love. He has blessed us with good health, love of God, and love of friends. It is God's plan for our salvation. This is why we learn to appreciate the little things we do for each other.

Robin: Then why do people spend so much time shopping and giving material gifts if God doesn't like it?

Mrs. Brown: Honey, God has nothing against giving gifts. In fact, He loves to see people giving, especially if they are giving out of love and concern, and have no thoughts or desires to receive gifts in return. You see, the joy of giving comes from the heart. Jesus taught us this in His word, and by His actions while He was here on earth.

Sandra: Robin, it's like loving to make people happy, especially at this time of the year. You do it for the joy of making others happy.

Robin: Okay, I think I get it now.

Mrs. Brown: I know I have kept you. But I want all of you to remember that the gift you gave to me and my daughter this evening is better than any material gift I could ever receive. And remember, if you have not received some special material gift, you will receive a greater gift from God. You came here and blessed my house with your beautiful voices. I now pray God's blessings upon each of you. *(She hugs each one of them)* Merry Christmas to all of you, and may God bless you always.

All: Merry Christmas to you!

Mike: And thanks for the cookies!

Robin: The way Mrs. Brown talks makes me all warm inside. I don't need any hot chocolate.

(They leave singing: Go, Tell It On The Mountain.*)*

The Town of Bethlehem 17

"While they were there, the time came for the baby to be born, and she gave birth to her firstborn, a son. She wrapped him in a cloth and placed him in a manger, because there was no room in the inn." Luke 2:6-7

The Town of Bethlehem

*

CHARACTERS

Narrator	Angel
Innkeeper	Cal
Joseph	Hannah
Mary	Joshua

4 Shepherds
3 Kings

Simeon	Anna

Children's Choir

3 Groups of Choral Readers

*Lights are dim. Children's choir members are dressed as angels and proceed down the center aisle with lighted candles. Soft piano music **"O Little Town Of Bethlehem".** When the choir is in place and candles are blown out, the narration begins. Soft music continues.*

Narrator O little town of Bethlehem – how could you ever guess what would happen within your boundaries during this eventful time? And you, Mary, could you ever imagine that you would become the mother of our Lord and Saviour Jesus Christ? Well, this is how it happened.

Mary was pledged to be married to Joseph. But before they came together, she was found to be with child through the Holy Spirit. When the time was near, Joseph and Mary, along with many others, traveled from Galilee to Bethlehem to register for the census, as Caesar Augustus had decreed. Let's join them!

Scene 1: *Bethlehem: A noisy crowd is entering the Inn. There is a small table for registration, a few chairs and tables with people sitting around them. Some are eating, drinking and talking very loudly. Others are coming. The Innkeeper is busy registering the crowd.*

Martha: Joshua, now that we have registered for the census, let's stay here tonight. I'm too tired to go another step.

Joshua: Okay by me. Who knows, there might be a party going on. Hey, here comes Cal!

Cal: Hey, Josh. You guys are speedsters. You got here before me. Are you leaving tonight?

Joshua: No. We just decided to stay and join the party. I believe it will be right here at the inn.

Hannah: Cal, let's stay. I am tired!

Cal: But what about the cattle? We need to get them in.

Hannah: They can graze on the hill for another day.

Cal: Okay. Hey, Innkeeper, can we have a room for the night?

Innkeeper: You're just in time, folks. I have only one more room left.

Hannah: We'll take it.

(Cal pays the Innkeeper. Joseph and Mary arrive. Mary remains a little distance away as Joseph goes up to talk with the Innkeeper)

Joseph: Sir, may we have a room for a night or two? My wife is with child, and ...

Innkeeper: I'm sorry, Sir, but I don't have a single room left.

Joseph: Oh my! Do you know where we might find a room in this town?

Innkeeper: Sir, I'm afraid all the places are just like mine, all filled up. You see, there are so many people because of the governor's decree. And those who have traveled a long way are staying the night.

Joseph: *(Looking down at Mary, distressed)* But Sir, my wife is about ready to deliver! What are we going to do?

Innkeeper: *(Yelling at the noisy crowd)* Hey! Keep it down, keep it down! I can't talk with these people! Come with me, Sir. Maybe I can arrange something.

(They move down to where Mary is standing)

Innkeeper: I can see that you do have a very urgent matter here. Listen, I have a stable around the corner where the animals feed. Maybe I could give you some blankets and you could stay there tonight.

Mary: That would be fine.

Innkeeper: Wait here. *(He leaves and soon returns with a bundle)* Here you are, Sir. Make her as comfortable as you can.

(Lights dim and the crowd quietly leaves the stage)

Song: O Little Town of Bethlehem: Choir sings verse 1

O little town of Bethlehem,
How still we see thee lie!
Above thy deep and dreamless sleep
The silent stars go by.

Yet in thy dark streets shineth
The everlasting Light
The hopes and fears of all the years
Are met in thee tonight.

Scene 2: *Narrator, Choral Readers 1 and 2 assemble.*

Narrator: God's people had been living in sin for so many years. Sometimes they were persuaded to follow Him, but soon they lost faith. God had tried many ways to bring them back and to forget their wicked ways. The coming of Christ, a Saviour for the world had been the prophecies of Isaiah, Jeremiah, Micah, and others whom the Lord had chosen to speak for Him. He promised this Messiah would bind up the wounds of the oppressed people, and show mercy to the downtrodden. This was good news for the people.

Choral Readers 1: Isaiah 9: 1b-2, 6-7a.

In the past He humbled the land of Zebulun and the land of Naphtali, but in the future He will honor Galilee of the Gentiles, by the way of the sea, along the Jordan. The people walking in darkness have seen a great light; on those living in the land of the shadow of death a light has dawned ...

For unto us a child is born, unto us a Son is given, and the government will be on his shoulders. And he will be called Wonderful, Counselor, Mighty God, Everlasting Father, Prince of Peace. Of the increase of his government and peace there will be no end ...

Choral Readers 2: Isaiah 42: 1-4a.

Here is my servant, whom I uphold, my chosen one in whom I delight. I will put my Spirit on him and he will bring Justice to the nations. He will not shout or cry out, or raise his voice in the streets. A bruised reed he will not break, and a smoldering wick he will not snuff out. In faithfulness he will bring forth justice; he will not falter or be discouraged till he establishes justice on earth.

(Lights dim and Choral Readers leave)

Song: O Come, O Come Emmanuel – Choir sings verse I and chorus.

O come, O come, Emmanuel
And ransom captive Israel,
That mourns in lonely exile here
Until the Son of God appears.

Rejoice! Rejoice! Emmanuel
Shall come to thee, O Israel

LOUD VOICE OFFSTAGE:

"Prepare ye the way of the Lord. Make straight in the desert a highway for our God. Every valley shall be exalted, and every mountain and hill shall be made low; and the crooked shall be straight, and the rough places plain. And the glory of the Lord shall be revealed, and all mankind shall see it together. For the mouth of the Lord has spoken it"

Scene 3: *Narrator and the Manger scene – Joseph, Mary and the Baby in the Manger.*

Narrator: The world prior to the birth of Christ was in a constant state of turmoil. People were worshiping different gods, and there was little hope for a real community of faith. Although His coming was prophesied for many years throughout the Old Testament times, few people ever expected Jesus' birth. Many thought He would be a king coming to them riding in a fine chariot in great splendor. No one would ever believe that He would be born in a stable, and of parents who lived in Galilee. Never!

(The star appears above the Manger)

Song: Away in a Manger – Choir sings verses I and 2

Away in a manger no crib for a bed,
The little Lord Jesus laid down His sweet head.
The stars in the sky looked down where He lay,
The little Lord Jesus, asleep on the hay.

The cattle are lowing, the Baby awakes,
But little Lord Jesus, no crying He makes;
I love Thee, Lord Jesus! Look down from the sky,
And stay by my cradle 'til morning is nigh.

Narrator: And there were shepherds in the same country abiding in the fields keeping watch over their flock by night.

(Shepherds enter and stop at a distance as they see the star)

1st Shep.: Look at that bright star. It seems to be moving with us!

2nd Shep.: Wow! I wonder why it is so much larger and brighter than the rest.

3rd Shep.: I don't know, but this is eerie! Maybe we should go back and hide in the hills!

(They turn around to leave, but an angel appears with outstretched arms)

Angel: Fear not, for behold, I bring you good tidings of great joy, which shall be to all people.

4th Shep.: What does this mean?

Angel: Unto you is born this day in the city of David, A Saviour, which is Christ the Lord!

1st Shep.: But what about that star?

Angel: *(Pointing to the star)* And this shall be a sign to you. You will find the babe wrapped in swaddling clothes, lying in a manger.

(Angel leaves quickly)

2nd Shep.: Let's go and see this thing that the Lord has made known to us.

(They moved slowly down to the manger and stared in awe at the baby, then raised their staffs in praises to God)

Soft music: O Little Town of Bethlehem.

3rd Shep.: Let's go and tell others what the Lord has shown us!

4th Shep.: Yes, let's hurry!

(They rushed off. The music grows louder, and Choral Readers 3 assemble)

Narrator: When King Herod heard the news that a King of the Jews had been born, he was furious, and began plotting secretly to find the exact time the star appeared. He sent the Magi to search for the child so he could destroy him, for he knew the people would remember the Prophecy of Micah.

Choral Readers 3: Micah 5:2-5.

But you, Bethlehem, though you are small among the clans of Judah, out of you will come for Me one who will be ruler over Israel, whose origins are from of old, from ancient times. Therefore, Israel will be abandoned until the time when she, who is in labor gives birth, and the rest of his brothers return to join the Israelites. He will stand and shepherd his flock in the strength of the Lord, in the majesty of the name of the Lord his God. And they will live securely, for then His greatness will reach to the ends of the earth. And He will be their peace.

Song: O Little Town of Bethlehem – Choir sings verse 4.

O Holy Child of Bethlehem,
Descend to us, we pray
Cast out our sins and enter in
Be born in us today.

We hear the Christmas angels
The great glad tidings tell;
O come to us, abide with us,
Our Lord Emmanuel!

Narrator: And the people came from far and near, bringing gifts for the newborn baby. Some had heard that He was the newborn King, and others were wondering if He would be the promised Messiah. If God was sending a King to earth, would He send Him to be born of a virgin, and in a stable?

(People come from all directions, carrying gifts to the manger for the baby. They move slowly. And far behind them, a little drummer boy comes beating upon his drum)

Narrator: Oh, look. Here comes a little boy playing on a drum!

Song: The Little Drummer Boy. Choir and gathering crowd sing all verses.

Narrator: Then there were the Kings from other countries who heard of the birth. They also knew that King Herod was angry, and was plotting to find and destroy the baby. They were excited and traveled to Bethlehem guided by the Star. When they saw the babe in the manger, they began to sing praises.

(The drumbeat continues as three Kings enter slowly and look at the baby)

Song: We Three Kings of Orient Are – Kings sing verse I – Choir joins in the refrain.

We three kings of Orient Are
  Bearing gifts we traverse afar,
Field and fountain, moor and mountain,
  Following yonder star.

O star of wonder, star of night
  Star with royal beauty bright,
Westward leading, still proceeding
  Guide us to thy perfect light.

Narrator: The Kings were so filled with joy and praise, they bowed before the manger, opened their bags and presented the babe with gifts of gold, frankincense, and myrrh. The Kings had been warned not to go back to Herod for they knew of his plot. So they went back to their country by another route.

(Music continues as the Kings leave)

Narrator: Now there was a righteous man in Jerusalem called Simeon who was filled with the Holy Spirit. The Spirit had revealed to him that he would not die before he had seen the Lord's Christ. He came to see the Holy Child, took him in his arms and lifted him high in praise.

(Simeon enters)

Simeon: Sovereign Lord, as you have promised, you now dismiss your servant in peace. For my eyes have seen your salvation.

(He speaks to Mary and Joseph)

The child is destined to cause the falling and rising of many in Israel, and the thoughts of many hearts will be revealed. A sword will pierce your own soul, also.

(He gives the baby back to Mary and leaves. Anna, the prophetess enters)

Narrator: There was also a prophetess named Anna, of the tribe of Asher. She was very old, and never left the temple, but worshipped night and day, fasting and praying. She came near, giving thanks to God for she knew this was the sign for the redemption of Jerusalem. She bowed her head for a moment and then slowly walked away.

Suddenly, Joseph remembered the angel of the Lord who came to him in a dream. He was warned to take the child and his mother and flee to Egypt so that Herod would not kill him. For Herod had ordered that all boys two years of age and under, in the vicinity of Bethlehem be killed. So Joseph and Mary took their baby and hurried away. What a wonderful time this was for the people of all nations!

Final Song: Go, Tell it on the Mountain – Choir will lead all verses and audience is asked to join in the refrain.

The End

Noah's Ark

A Drama based on Genesis Chapters 6-8

"The animals going in were male and female of every living thing, as God had commanded Noah ..."

Genesis 7:16

NOAH'S ARK

was written for the
Charles G. Adams Drama Group
Of
Hartford Memorial Baptist Church.
It was performed more than once over
the years in the history of this organization.

Noah's Ark
Is presented
In memory of the late
Simonetta Zenobia Smith,
Co-founder of the
CGA Drama Group
With Pastor Charles G. Adams
(Organized in 1974)

Noah's Ark

CHARACTERS

Narrator
Voice of God
Noah
Shem
Ham
Japheth
Noah's Wife
Shem's Wife
Ham's Wife
Japheth's Wife
3 to 5 Hecklers
Singers

Animals (Costumes)

Costumes by
________Cora Pearson________

Music Director
________Donald R. Johnson________

Directed by
Omega Flowers

This play is based on the biblical account found in Genesis sixth through the eighth chapters. It is my prayer that this will be yet another inspiring presentation challenging young people to learn more about God's love and purpose for His people.

ACT ONE

(The stage is dark. Spotlight is on the narrator)

Narrator: Good evening, Christian friends. We are happy to have you join us tonight on our journey into the pages of biblical history. We ask now that you open your Bibles and minds as we explore chapters six through eight of Genesis. Here you will find the story of Noah and the flood. Now the generations of man had begun to increase rapidly, according to God's plan. But as they did, immorality and lewd behavior were becoming a way of life. Man seemed to have lost all respect for himself and for God. As we read the pages, we cannot help feeling that even now, we are re-living the times of Noah.

Our Lord was angered by man's display of sin and corruption, and rightly so. For He had made this creature in his own image. He scooped the dust from the ground, molded it in the palm of His hands, and breathed into it the breath of life. And now it seemed that the light of our Lord's miraculous creature had grown dim. But, in the midst of sin and corruption, God found one man who was a just and perfect man, and He began to work with him.

Voice Of God: Wicked! Wicked! Wicked! My people have brought shame upon me. Sin is corrupting my creation. I will destroy man. I will banish him from the face of the earth. I will destroy man and all beast with him, for I now regret that I have made them.

(Spotlight is on Noah as he enters slowly)

But there is one ... There is one in whom I have found favor.

(He calls in a loud voice) Noah! Noah! I am the Lord thy God.

(Noah is frightened and falls to his knees)

It grieves me that this earth which I have created has become violent and corrupt. Man has disobeyed me. He has forgotten that I created him. I shall destroy man. I shall destroy this earth and every living creature therein.

(Noah covers his head as if to hide from God)

All but thee and thine, Noah. For you have fellowshipped with me in spite of this horrible and sinful world. Listen, and I will establish my covenant with thee, for thou art a just and perfect man.

Noah: *(Raises his arms)* Thank you, my Lord. But how shall this be?

Voice Of God: I want you to build an ark. Build it 300 cubits long, 50 cubits wide, and 30 cubits high. There should be 3 stories with rooms so that your sons and their wives and all thy house may dwell within. Pitch it with tar within and without so that it will weather the storm. For in a few days, I will bring a great flood to the land. Rushing waters and wind will destroy all flesh, men and beast, and even the fowl of the air.

Noah: *(He gets to his feet)* But, my Lord ...

Voice Of God: Yes, Noah. Once the ark is completed, take into it all thine household. Take also two of every living thing, beast, fowl, clean and unclean, male and female, so that after the flood we may replenish the earth. Get busy

Noah, for in a few days, I will send the waters from heaven to cleanse the filth from this earth.

(Spotlight goes out and stage lights up. Noah begins rushing around)

Noah: Shem! Ham! Japheth! Come quickly, we have work to do.

(The three men rush in)

We must build an ark – a great ship. For the Lord will destroy the earth very soon now. The rains will come and continue until the earth is covered with water, and all living things will drown.

All Men Together: What?

Noah: Yes, and we must hurry. God gave me a plan to follow.

Shem: But, Father!

Noah: God has spoken to me, my son.

Ham: *(Gestures with both arms)* Rain! Flood! Death! Father, could you be mistaken?

Noah: No, my son. God came to me in this place. I talked with Him as I have many times before. He laid the plans before me. It is so.

Shem: Okay, Father.

Japheth: But do we have enough time? This sounds like a big job.

Noah: Yes, Japheth. If it were not so, God would have instructed me.

(They begin to work, pulling boards and other objects to center stage. Noah begins to sing)

It's gonna rain, chillin'
God's gonna send the water from Zion,
It's gonna raise the heavens up higher,
It's gonna rain!

(The sons join in the singing, and they sing it over and over as they work)

Shem: *(Walking around and looking up)* Father, the clouds seem to be forming. How long do we have before the rains come?

Noah: We have enough time, my son. We will work steadily day and night. I'm sure it will be ready.

(The sons take turns singing separately, then together they harmonize)

Ham: *(Worrying)* Father, how long can we survive in a ship like this? Suppose the storm is a rough one!

Noah: Hush, man! God speaks to me, and I have no doubt that He is in control. Work!

(They begin hammering as the curtains close)

Singers Offstage:

Have faith in God
Have faith in God
Have faith in God for deliverance
Have faith, have faith in God.

My faith looks up to Thee,
Thou Lamb of Calvary;
Saviour, Divine
Now hear me while I pray,
Take all my guilt away;

Have faith in God for deliverance,
Have faith, have faith in God.

(When the curtains open, a pre-built structure is in place. Noah and his sons are on stage)

Noah: Well, this looks sturdy enough!

Ham: Father, I'm sorry I doubted. It just seemed so impossible at the time.

Noah: That's all right, son. Go now and tell your wives to pack food for storing. Tell them to empty the cupboards and bring all they have, for we have a long journey ahead of us.

Shem: Yes, Father.

Noah: And tell them not to worry. The Lord has spoken to me, and His word is faithful and true. We will be safe.

(The sons leave. Noah remains examining the ship. Soon singing is heard offstage)

Singers Offstage:

Great is Thy faithfulness! Great is Thy
faithfulness! Morning by morning new
mercies I see.
All I have needed Thy hands hath
provided; Great is Thy faithfulness
Lord unto me!

(Noah leaves. A few minutes later the sons' wives enter carrying bags and boxes and placing them inside the Ark)

Shem's Wife: Do you think Noah knows what he is talking about?

Ham's Wife: I don't know. I wonder about Noah sometimes.

Japheth's Wife: My husband believes in his father; and I must believe in him, also.

(Noah's wife enters carrying a large box)

Noah's Wife: I couldn't help overhearing your conversation. I know sometimes it's hard to believe. *(She moves from one to the other placing her hands on their shoulders)* As long as I have known Noah, even before we were married, Noah has walked with God. You only have to see the peace and comfort he gets when he prays. We must believe in him. *(Noah enters carrying supplies. Hecklers come by laughing and poking fun at Noah's Ark)*

1st Heckler: Look! What are they building?

2nd: It must be some kind of a house, or a boat.

3rd: If that's a house, then old man Noah has really flipped his lid!

(They all laugh)

4th: Hey, Mr. Noah! Who's going to live in that funny looking house?

1st: Is your god coming to live with you?

2nd: Now you got me wondering; what does his god look like?

3rd: Probably looks like a sea monster. Who else would live in such a monstrosity?

4th: Yeah! They're all a bunch of weirdos!

(Noah rushes over with a stick and chases them away)

Noah: If they only knew what is in store for them. They would not be laughing.

Ham's Wife: I hope we have enough food and supplies. This flood could last for a long time.

Noah: Don't worry, my children. God will take care of us.

(The ladies all leave. Noah raises his arms in praise to God, and sings)

The Lord will provide,
The Lord will provide.

O, somehow, some way, or other
I know the Lord will provide.

I've had so many problems,
I've had trouble on every side;
But somehow, some way, or other
I know the Lord will provide.

CURTAINS

ACT TWO

(As the curtains open, Noah and his sons are inspecting the Ark. The wives come in carrying more bags and boxes. Thunder and lightning begin, and grow louder and louder)

Noah: This should keep us safe and dry during the storm.

Ham: Thank God, it is finished.

Shem: Are the portholes sealed, Japheth?

Japheth: Yes, and I have double-checked all the latches.

Noah: Go now and fetch the animals – the beast of the fields and the fowl of the air, for thus saith the Lord.

(All leave except Noah and his wife. The storm grows louder. Some people stagger by with their heads covered and cloaks pulled tightly around them)

1st Person — Mr. Noah, please may we come inside from the storm?

2nd — Please take us in. We have no place to go!

3rd — Our homes have been destroyed. Please, may we come in?

4th — Oh please, Mr. Noah. We cannot survive in this storm. We will all perish.

5th — We will pay. You may have all our earthly possessions. Just let us come in until the storm is over.

(Loud thunder frightens them and they run out.. The men and women bring in the animals. Lights are dim. Finally all are safely aboard)

Singers Offstage:

When peace like a river, attendeth my way;
When sorrows like sea billows roll;
Whatever my lot, Thou hast taught me to
say, It is well, it is well, with my soul.

It is well, with my soul. It is well, it is well,
with my soul. *(Repeat)*

(When the curtains open, the scene is inside the Ark. The men are lying around sleeping)

Ham's Wife: *(Walks around holding her hands up)* I never knew so much water could fall from the sky!

Shem's Wife: The Ark was finished just in time, thanks be to God.

Japheth's Wife: I wonder how long this will last!

(Noah's wife walks over and places a blanket over Noah who has fallen asleep on the floor)

Noah's Wife: The men worked hard and for many long hours. Noah is so tired. I thought at one time he would give up, but God is with Noah. This is why he can sleep so peacefully now.

(The all seat themselves and seemingly fall asleep)

Singers Offstage:

When the storms of life are raging, stand by me.
When the storms of life are raging, stand by me;
When the world is tossing me like a ship upon the sea
Thou who rulest wind and water, stand by me.

In the midst of tribulations, stand by me;
In the midst of tribulations, stand by me;
When the host of hell assail, and my strength begins to fail; Thou who never lost a battle, stand by me.

Narrator: And so it was that Noah and all that abideth in the Ark were lifted up on surges of waves, and floated along without a sail or a propeller; up and up as the waters continued to rise. And the days and nights passed without much attention to time or cares. Noah's confidence seems to have settled in tranquil serenity over all the Ark's inhabitants; so much so that men and beast dozed as if they were being rocked in a cradle of love and protection. God's family of men and beast rested in His hands.

Singers Offstage:

He's got the whole world in His hands;
He's got the whole world in His hands;
He's got the whole world in His hands;
He's got the whole world in His hands.

(The family begins to awake from sleep)

Shem: Oh boy! What a dream I had! I wonder what the world will look like when the flood is over.

Ham: It seems that we have been in this box forever. Whatever it looks like will be a welcome sight for me.

Japheth: Just think, we could be miles away from our old homestead.

Shem: I won't care about the strangeness of the land. I will just be happy to settle on "dry" land again!

(Japheth's wife picks up a small animal and caresses it)

Singers Offstage: He's got the little bitty baby in His hands;
He's got the little bitty baby in His hands;
He's got the little bitty baby in His hands;
He's got the whole world in His hands.

Narrator: And the Ark floated on and on. And Noah made the rounds, checking the latches for soundness. Suddenly, through a small porthole, Noah saw a light. Excitedly, he rushed over and got the raven and released it through the tiny window. Then he explained to his sons that if the water was receding, the bird would bring back a sign. But the raven did not return. And Noah sent out a dove, and then another. It seems that Noah's hurried movement stirred even the animals. Noah opened the hatch a little wider and found that the rain had stopped. He turned with outstretched arms acknowledging victory.

Singers Offstage: Take courage my soul, and let us journey on,
Tho' the night be dark, it won't be very long.

Thanks be to God, the morning light appear; The storm is passing over, the storm is passing over, the storm is passing over, Halleluia.
See the lightening flashing, the billows touch the ground. Hear the thunder rolling, there's darkness all around. Thanks be to God, the morning light appears. The storm is passing over; the storm is passing over; the storm is passing over, Halleluia.

Narrator: It wasn't long before victory came, for the dove Noah sent out returned with an olive twig in its beak. The flood was over and the water had receded from the face of the earth. When the Ark came to rest on land and Noah and all who were with him came out, they saw the rainbow and knew that God had made a covenant with all mankind. He sent them out to be fruitful and replenish the earth.

(As the curtains close, the rainbow is projected on them)

Narrator: And so it was in the days of Noah, that faith was restored in mankind. And so it is in our lives today. Think back to the greatest storm in your life and reflect for a moment on how the sun came through when you turned it all over to Jesus. We are witnessing tonight that there is a key in our lives to the goodness of God. And that key is obedience and prayer.

Let us pray: Almighty God, your children have attempted to bring history and our roots a little bit closer to us tonight. And it is only by your grace that we have this opportunity. We thank you for your word. We have studied your grace and mercy through the experiences of Noah. We pray that whatever we have done here will be a blessing to someone. Thank you for those who came, and keep us together as a family just as you kept Noah and his family. This is our prayer in Jesus' name. Amen.

THE END

The Witnesses

A drama that teaches character building
to young people

"Speak and act as those who are going to be judged by the law that gives freedom, because judgment without mercy will be shown to anyone who has not been merciful. Mercy triumphs over judgment!"
James 2:12-13

The Witnesses

CHARACTERS

A group of High School students

Jill
Joyce
Monica
Susan
Bob
Paul
Tom

Two daughters of the store owner
Greta and Paula

Store Owner
Mr. Munson

Two young children
Jimmy and Val

Two Policemen

Paul 2

Jesus

SCENE 1: *The alley near Paul Brown's house. Paul rushes in and hides behind a barrel. Two Policemen come along with billy clubs searching for him. Finally, they give up and leave the scene. Paul comes out just as Bob and Tom enter. Bob has a ball and Tom has a bat.*

Bob: Hi, Paul. We're going down to city park and play ball. 'Wanna come along?

Paul: No. I have to be at home in a few minutes.

Tom: Aw, come on, Paul. We just saw your Mom leaving for her church meeting. She'll be gone at least two hours. You'll be home by then.

Bob: Besides, we need a pitcher. You know Cary can't pitch.

Tom: Yeah. We always lose when he pitches!

Paul: Sorry, fellas. I gotta go. *(He rushes off)*

Bob: Boy, he sure is nervous today. You think he's in trouble again?

Tom: Could be! He's always in trouble. You can't get that guy to go straight.

Bob: I know! I gave up on him a long time ago. Let's go.

(Mr. Munson rushes in)

Munson: Wait, fellas! Have you seen Paul Brown today? That good-for-nothing thief just stole an expensive radio from my store!

(Bob and Tom look at each other)

Bob: Mr. Munson, how do you know it was Paul?

Munson: Who else steals around here? Last month he took a clock from the counter. And before that, an electric shaver. His Dad brought back the shaver, but ...

Tom: Did you report this to the police?

Munson: Of course I did! And this time I will press charges no matter what his father says. That good for nothing bum should be behind bars.

(Munson leaves. Susan and Joyce enters)

Susan: What's all the excitement about? Mr. Munson looks like he is fighting a lion!

Bob: He claims Paul just stole a radio from his store.

Joyce: We just saw Paul running down the alley towards his house. I just knew he was in trouble again!

Susan: But, Joyce, Paul didn't have anything in his hands. If he just stole it, where was it?

Joyce: He must have hidden it some place; probably in a garbage can until he can come back and get it.

Susan: Did Mr. Munson say he saw Paul take the radio?

Tom: He didn't say. He's mad. But Paul is slick. He could steal the seams out of your pocket and you wouldn't catch him!

Susan: You know, I talked with Paul last week, and he said he has changed. He really wants to turn his life around. I believe him.

Bob: He was at church last Sunday, and that's unusual.

Susan: I invited him to Youth Fellowship last Friday, but he didn't come.

Joyce: Oh! He was outside the church when I came in. I spoke to him. He just asked where I was going.

Susan: Why didn't you invite him in?

Joyce: What for? He's not our kind. I don't think he even joined the church yet. And he probably was the one who took my 10-speed last summer.

Tom: Aw, Joyce. You're just mad because he never made a play for you. Let's go, Bob.

(Bob and Tom leave)

Joyce: Mad! I have nothing to be mad about. And as far as a "play" is concerned, I don't need that kind of attention. I'm talking to Jerry now, anyway.

Susan: Joyce, how quickly you forget that God teaches in Matthew 7:1: "Judge not, that ye be not judged". We just studied that last week. When we judge, accuse, and condemn one another, we are doing the work of the devil.

Joyce: I'm not judging him! If the guy has tripped out, it's not my fault!

(Jill and Monica enter)

Jill: Hey, Susan, Joyce – you're missing all the excitement. Paul's mother is down at Munson's store, and they are really getting it on!

Monica: Yes, Mr. Munson went to the church looking for Mrs. Brown and accusing Paul of stealing from his store.

Susan: What?

Joyce: Hey, let's go. I want to catch this action!

(Jill, Joyce and Monica leave. Susan sits down, bows her head and prays aloud)

Susan: O, Lord! You know the hearts and tongues of your children because you made us. Paul and his family are in need of your mercy and love right now. Please come to their rescue. Amen.

CURTAINS

Scene 2: *In front of Munson's store. Mr. Munson is discussing the situation with his daughters Greta and Paula. Jill, Joyce and Monica arrive.*

Paula: The nerve of that woman. You can tell she is covering for her son.

Munson: If I weren't a gentleman, I would have physically thrown her out of my store. She knows her son is a thief!

Greta: But Father, she did say Paul was home cleaning the garage this morning. That was about the time the radio disappeared.

Paula: How would she know? She was at church.

Joyce: So the thief hasn't been caught yet!

Greta: Joyce, please!

Munson: Don't worry. I'll get him. He can't hide forever. *(He pounds the table)* Where are the police? I called them almost an hour ago!

Greta: Don't worry, Father. *(She tries to console him, but he storms out)*

Monica: Did Mrs. Brown say where Paul is now?

Paula: She didn't say, but he's probably hiding somewhere right there in their house.

Jill: She is insisting that he did not steal the radio.

Paula: I don't believe that. Everybody knows Paul steals, even from his own parents. Remember when he got caught trying to hock his mother's watch?

Joyce: How could I forget. He promised to take me to the movies that night. I found out later he took Sarah Cannon, the little witch!

Greta: How do you know the watch belonged to his mother?

Paula: Or the time Joe said Paul took the tires off his bike to replace his own worn out ones.

Monica: Joe and Paul were supposed to be the best of friends.

Joyce: I know.

Jill: Oh yes, and remember the Science teacher's purse? Paul was the only one close to her desk.

Greta: Now, wait just a minute. You guys didn't see Paul take any of these things. It seems you are condemning him on 'hearsay', and that's wrong.

Paula: Just listen to you, little sister. It sounds like you're defending the thief!

Greta: No, I'm not. I'm just trying to get you to see that your gossip is not based on facts. You didn't see him take any of those things. Just like none of you were even here when the radio was taken.

Jill: Oh, Greta. Where have you been all our lives?

Monica: Yeah! You can look at that guy and tell he is a crook. He never looks you straight in the eye.

Greta: I don't believe you! How can you convict Paul without hearing his defense? You are witnessing to 'hearsay'. That's wrong!

Paula: But, Greta, we got these facts from the horse's mouth. Now why would our friends lie on Paul?

Jill: Yes. And after all, we need to know who to trust and who not to trust. So that's why we have to discuss it.

Greta: Do any of you remember the 9th commandment?

Monica: Oh please, Greta!

Greta: What is it, Monica?

Monica: Okay! "Thou shalt not bear false witness against thy neighbor". But, Greta ...

Greta: Do you know what that means?

Joyce: We know! We know!

Greta: God gave us this commandment in order that we will guard the rights and reputation of others. He meant for us to confine our words to that which we <u>know</u> is true.

Joyce: Okay! Watch out for Greta. She's now pulling the 'goody, goody' act on us.

Jill: Yes, and her father's store was just robbed. Save that for Friday, Greta.

(Two policemen enter)

Police #1: Did any of you see what happened at this store today?

(They all look at each other)

Police #2: Have you seen Paul Brown today?

Joyce: Well, I saw two friends down the street earlier and Paul had just left them. They said ...

Police #1: They said what, young lady?

Joyce: I meant, they said he had just left going home.

Police #2: Did you know that he is accused of stealing something from Munson's store?

Jill: We heard! *(sarcastically)*

Greta: We were just discussing the theft. But none of us saw anything. Please come with me. My father wishes to talk with you.

(Greta and the policemen leave)

Paula: I, for one will be glad to see Paul get what's coming to him. If he stole the radio, he should be punished.

Joyce: I hope Mr. Munson knows if he needs a witness in court, just call me. I can tell them a thing or two. They need to know about this slippery guy. When I finish, he'll be sorry he forgot to pick me up for the picnic two weeks ago.

Monica: Joyce, you never told us you were dating Paul.

Jill: Was he trying to borrow his uncle's car to take you to the picnic?

Joyce: Borrow! More than likely he would have stolen it!

(They all laugh)

Monica: Let's go. We'll see Greta at Friday night's Fellowship.

(They leave. Two children, Jimmy and Val, come on stage carrying a radio)

Jimmy: Hey, Val! Where did you get this? It's a beauty.

Val: It doesn't belong to me. I borrowed it from my brother Tony's room. I think he just got it today. It was in the back of his closet.

Jimmy: Boy, this is super!

Val: He doesn't know I have it. So when you see him, keep your big mouth shut!

Jimmy: Okay. Let's play it.

Val: See! It has a tape recorder and a microphone. Let's record something.

Jimmy: What will we record? Why don't you sing, and I'll be the DJ.

Val: Cool! You get it started. I'm ready.

Jimmy: There. "And now for your listening pleasure, Val will sing". You're on!

(Val sings as the curtains close)

Scene 3: *Susan is still with her head bowed. Paul comes quietly, looking around to see if he is being watched)*

Susan: *(Looks up, startled)* Oh, Paul! I didn't hear you coming!

Paul: Susan, I'm glad you're here. I need to talk with someone.

Susan: Okay, I'm here for you.

Paul: I know you heard about the theft at Mr. Munson's store.

Susan: Yes, I did.

Paul: Susan, I didn't take anything. I was home cleaning the garage all morning. I heard some kids coming down the alley talking about Mr. Munson's store being robbed. I just knew I would be accused.

Susan: O, Paul. How terrible!

Paul: I went down the street to see if I could find out what was stolen. I met Tony. He said Mr. Munson was looking for me because I had stolen a radio from his store.

Susan: How did Tony know?

Paul: I don't know. I didn't ask him. I only knew I had to get out of sight for awhile.

Susan: So what did you do?

Paul: I saw Bob and Tom. They tried to get me to go with them to play ball. Oh God, I wish I had gone. Then I would have had an alibi.

Susan: But you said you were cleaning the garage.

Paul: I was. But nobody saw me there. Anyway, after I heard the news. I went home and locked the door.

Susan: Paul, I believe you. I remember you started to tell me about your change.

Paul: Oh yes, that Sunday you saw me at church. Well, that night I went home and prayed to God to help me change my life. I have felt guilty for a long time, and I didn't like the feeling.

Susan: Go on.

Paul: I don't know why I just kept on doing bad things, stealing, lying, cheating. And after I did these things, I went home and had terrible sick feelings in my stomach.

Susan: How awful for you, Paul. But why didn't you talk with someone? You could have gone to Rev. Michaels, or come to me, or to Greta.

Paul: I don't know. I was ashamed. But after I went home from church, I stayed in my room for the rest of the day wondering what I would do.

Susan: Go on.

Paul: Anyway, after I knew my folks had gone to bed, I got on my knees tried to talk with God. I didn't know what I would say but ...

(Lights dim and scene changes to two figures in the background)

Paul 2: Lord, show me the way. Lord show me how to change. I don't want to do these bad things, but I don't seem to know how to stop.

Jesus: I am here, my son. I hear you.

Paul 2: Lord, I have sinned against you and against so many people.

Jesus: But all mankind has sinned and come short of my glory. I came not to call the righteous, but sinners to repentance.

Paul 2: Lord, show me how to repent. I don't want to continue my life as a sinner. How can I change? My friends won't believe me, or accept me.

Jesus: My child, do not despair. Because thou hast asked

these things, behold, I have done according to your words. Blessed is He whose transgression is forgiven. For the Lord thy God is a jealous God. Blessed is he who repents of his sins.

Paul 2: But how shall I convince people I have changed?

Jesus: Whatsoever things ye desire, when ye pray, believe that ye receive them, and ye shall have them. Goodbye, my son.

Paul 2: Thank you, Lord.

(Two figures move off stage and the lights brighten again)

Paul: Susan, I can't explain, nor will I ever forget what happened to me that night. I feel so good about it. But I still don't know how to beat this rap with Mr. Munson. I am scared!

Susan: Paul, I don't think you have to worry about that. Remember, whatsoever you desire, ask the Lord, and it will be given unto you.

CURTAINS

Scene 4: *Friday night Fellowship. All are seated on stage. Greta, the president is standing before them.*

Greta: Good evening to all of you. Tonight we will deviate a little from our usual program in order to reflect upon the happenings of this week. Some of you may wish to say something in that regard. I do want you to know that the mystery of the stolen radio from my father's store is over.

(Applause)

Before we begin, I have asked Monica to read a poem.

Monica: I believe the title of this poem should be "Has Someone Seen Christ In Your Life Today":

Has someone seen Christ in your life today?
Christians, look to your heart, I pray.
The little things you have done and said,
Did they accord with the way you prayed?
Have your thoughts been pure and words been
kind? Have you sought to have the Savior's
Mind?
The world with a criticizing view
Has watched; but did it see Christ in you?

Has someone seen Christ in you today?
Christian, look to your life, I pray;
There are aching hearts and blighted souls
Being lost on sin's destructive roads.
And perhaps of Christ their only view
May be what they see of Christ in you.
Will they see enough to bring hope and cheer?
Look to your light! Does it shine out clear?

(Silence)

Greta: Susan will now pray.

Susan: Almighty God, our father; Creator of the heavens and the earth. Creator of the living creatures, and creator of us all. We praise you for your creation. We praise you for your plan for our salvation through Jesus Christ. We ask for guidance and your tender mercy. Forgive us, Lord, this day for our sins against Thee and against our brother. Forgive our selfishness, conceit, and our sins of gossiping and accusing. We ask, O God, that you search our hearts always to show love and compassion toward one another. All these things we ask in the name of your Son, Jesus Christ. Amen.

Greta: I want to thank those of you who have been praying with us this week. As you know, our store was robbed, but thanks to God, the robber was caught. We are so glad to have Paul with us tonight who must have spent many tough hours. But God is Good.

(Greta sits)

Paula: We are glad the thief was caught, but it didn't happen before a lot of damage had been done through a lot of gossiping and accusing. I shared in all of this, and I am truly sorry. I have asked God's forgiveness, and Paul, I hope you will forgive me, too.

Jill: Paul, I am glad you are with us. We were terrible. Instead of reaching out to help you, we condemned you with our foolishness. I am sorry!

Joyce: I guess I did more damage than anyone. I don't know how I could have been so stupid. I only hope you will forgive me. I was ready to witness to something I knew nothing about, when I should have been a witness for God and His goodness. Please forgive me!

Val: I could have told you guys Paul didn't steal that radio. But who listens to a little kid? My stupid brother Tony stole it. Now I need you guys to pray for him.

Greta: We will pray for Tony, Val. Welcome to Youth Fellowship, Paul. Let me leave this thought with all of us. Romans 14, verse 13 says, "Let us not therefore judge one another anymore, but judge this rather, that no man put a stumbling block or an occasion to fall in his brother's way".

ALL: Amen.

Paul: I want to thank all of you for your concern and prayers. God is good. Anytime He can change a poor guy like me, I believe He can do anything. I am a witness tonight to a personal encounter with God. He showed me the alternative to sin and all the mean things I have done. I thank you for accepting me, but my most sincere thanks go to God. I want you to know that I could never condemn you for your actions, "for all have sinned and come short of the glory of God". Thank you again.

THE END

The Triumphal Entry

A Parade for the Common People

Jesus was celebrated a King, but rode
into Jerusalem on a donkey instead
of in a chariot

CAST

2 Narrators

Children: Andrew, Beth, Bob, John, Mary, Michael, Ruth, Susan, Tommy

Apostle Peter

King Jesus

The Crowd: As many as can be gathered out of sight. They can be heard chanting, singing, and cheering. And then they follow Peter.

Song Leader

PROPS

Sound Tracks: A walking horse
Noise of the crowd

Palm branches

Narrator 1: Six days before the Passover began, Jesus arrived in Bethany where He found Lazarus. When people of Jerusalem heard of His arrival, they came in crowds to see Him, and to see the man who had been raised from the dead. This troubled the Jews because many in their own ranks had started following Jesus after seeing other miracles.

Narrator 2: The next day, the news that Jesus was on his way to Jerusalem swept through the city, and large crowds of Passover visitors pressed their way along the road to get a glimpse of Him. They broke palm branches and scattered them along the road. There was a strange air of excitement throughout the city and the countryside.

(Bob, Susan and Mary enter)

Bob: Why are all these people coming to Jerusalem?

Susan: My mom says they are gathering for the Feast of the Passover.

Mary: You know, people are always coming her for something. But this time it's a little different. The excitement is every where.

Susan: That's because Jesus of Nazareth, who claims to be the Messiah, is coming!

(Beth, John and Tommy enter excitedly)

Tommy: Hey, you guys! A big crowd is coming! See the cloud of dust down the road?

(They all stand. While they were standing and talking, the noise of the crowd grew louder. People were chanting "Hosanna" and cheering)

Beth: My brother John and I heard the excitement and we ran ahead so we could see.

John: Yes. Jesus visited Lazarus. You know, the man who was dead and came back to life!

Susan: My mom said Jesus performed a miracle and brought Lazarus back to life.

Beth: I'll bet Lazarus is coming with Him. I want to see the man who was dead and is living again.

Susan: I want to see Jesus! I overheard some people talking. He really sounds like a King!

Mary: I wish I could make a crown for His head. A King should always wear a crown.

Tommy: If He is truly a King, his crown will cost a fortune, and you won't be able to afford the material to make it.

Bob: My parents said Jesus is a carpenter. How can he be made a King so fast?

Beth: I understand that no man on this earth appointed Him King. He got His commission from a higher source. from God Himself.

Susan: Yes. God almighty crowned Him King, and that's the highest authority!

(John moves closer to the edge of stage as horse's hoofs grow louder)

John: Listen! The crowd is getting closer!

(Michael, Andrew and Ruth rushes in)

Michael: Hey, you guys! You should see the people coming along the road!

Andrew: Yes! There are thousands of them! They're breaking branches from the palm trees and scattering them all along the road!

Ruth: I was asleep, and my cousin came bursting in shouting "Jesus is coming, Jesus is coming'.

Michael: You think we can see them from here?

Susan: If we stand on these benches, maybe we can see Him as He passes by.

Mary: I just wonder – there is a lot of talk going on about Jesus. My father is a member of the Sanhedrin Court, and I've heard things that make me feel scared!

Bob: You're right. For instance, if He has a record of saving people from all kinds of sicknesses and diseases, why won't all the people believe in Him?

Andrew: Well, there is so much secrecy. I just want to see Him. I think I am a pretty good judge of character.

All: Booooo! *(mocking Andrew)*

Mary: If I only knew what was going on! All this makes me scared!

Tommy: Look! Here they come. Hush, they are singing.

(Jesus is on a donkey, but the crowd is flanked around Him so only his head and shoulders are visible. They are moving slowly. Peter is ahead of them and a larger crowd follows.. He is leading them in the chanting)

Peter: Behold! The King is coming.

Crowd: *(Chanting)* Hosanna! Blessed is He that cometh in the name of the Lord.

Peter Rejoice greatly O Jerusalem!

Crowd: Blessed is He that cometh in the name of the Lord!

Peter: Hosanna to the Son of David!

Crowd: Blessed is He that cometh in the name of the Lord!

Peter: Behold, the King. Save now, O King!

Crowd: Save us, O Lord!

Peter: *(Raises his hands and stops the movement of the crowd)* Arise, O Jerusalem and meet your King!

Song Leader *raises hands signaling audience to stand and join in singing:*

Blessed be the Name, Blessed be the Name
Blessed be the Name of the Lord
Blessed be the Name, Blessed be the Name
Blessed be the Name of the Lord

(Repeat)

(Song Leader signals the audience of be seated)

Narrator 1: Peter has been leading this crowd all the way. One can only wonder if Pilate is watching, and what is going on in his mind. The situation inside the city is growing tense as the hours pass. Wait! Jesus is speaking!

Jesus: "O Jerusalem, O Jerusalem. If I had known this day the things which belonged to your peace. But now they are hidden from your eyes. The day shall come when your enemies shall cast a trench about you, and keep you on every side. And shall lay you even with the ground. And your children with you. The time is now, that I must return to my father. And I say unto you, if you love your life down here, you will lose it. But if you despise your life down here you will exchange it for eternal glory."

(Jesus and the flanking crowd leave slowly. Music: Blessed be the Name is being played softly on the piano)

Narrator 2: There is no question about it. Jesus, the carpenter, now hailed "King" is making history today. He is riding on a donkey, flanked by his closest friends, the apostles. His popularity has grown, and the crowd has tripled since we caught up with Him. The guards who were waiting to stop Him have decided there is no chance of halting the procession at this point. Jesus of Nazareth is now inside the city.

CURTAINS

As the curtains are closing, Song Leader signals the audience to join in singing more verses of Blessed Be The Name

The Prodigal Son

A Drama based on Luke 15:11-31

"But while he was still a long way off, his father saw him and was filled with compassion for him; he ran to his son, threw his arms around him and kissed him".

Luke 15:20

The Prodigal Son

CHARACTERS

Father
Mother
Amos
Elam – *The Prodigal*
Lyla - *Maid*
Jenny - *Maid*
Jason – *Servant*
Jude - *Servant*
Child – *8 years old*
Sister – *6 years old*
Brother – *5 years old*
Traveler
Traveler's wife

Scene 1: The living room of a farm house. Father sits with his arms on a table, seemingly deep in thought. Mother sits nearby. She is knitting.

Father: You know, Dear, we are getting old now. Soon God will see fit to take us from this place where we have had such a good life.

Mother: Why are you talking of things yet to come? Are you not feeling well?

Father: As strong as the cattle that graze upon that hillside over there *(pointing towards the window).*

Mother: Then what troubles you?

Father: I was thinking about our two sons. They are both good men, but sometimes I just think they are so different, and not close as brothers should be.

Mother: *(Places her knitting in the basket beside her and looks seriously at him)* Remember when they were young and I did all the worrying? I was worrying if they were cold at night, or if they would come home safe from their hunting trips. You scolded me!

Father: I know, Dear. It's just that our youngest son seems so restless and short of temper. Haven't you noticed?

Mother: No. But you are with them much more than I am. I pray constantly for them. They are strong men, and God will keep them strong.

(Maids Lyla and Jenny enter)

Lyla: My lady, there's a little kid at the back door begging for bread. What shall I do with him?

Mother: I'll come and see.

(Mother and Father leave. The servants tidy the room. They did not notice the child who sneaked in and hid behind the chair)

Lyla: She should let me send him away. When I finish with the little devil, he wouldn't think about coming around here again!

Jenny: Isn't he the same child that Jason caught taking apples from the barrel outside last week?

Lyla: Probably so. These kids will steal your shirt if they get a chance!

Jenny: *(Sees the child who has crawled under the table)* Hey! What are you doing under that table?

(The child stands up looking frightened and yells at them)

Child: This ain't your house. I can come here if I want to!

Lyla: But you come here to steal stuff!

(He grabs an apple from the table)

Child: So what? I only take something for my brother and sister. They are hungry all the time!

Lyla: *(Starts toward him)* Get out of here, you little thief! What do you think you are doing?

Child: Listen, you old biddy; Mr. Amos gives me whatever I want when I come over here. What's your problem?

Jenny: But you haven't seen Mr. Amos today! He doesn't know what you are doing!

Child: He told me yesterday I could come back today if I wanted to.

(He grabs another apple and stuffs it in a bag he has behind his back)

Lyla: Hey, you came in here to steal. What else do you have in that bag?

(They try to catch him again)

Child: You leave me alone. I'm gonna tell Mr. Amos how you are treating me! I'm going home and tell my momma, too.

Jenny: Where do you live?

Child: None of your business!

(He grabs more fruit from the table and runs out)

Lyla: Can you beat that? He's a nervy little devil!

(Father enters)

Jenny: Anything we can do for you, Sir?

Father: No. I just want to sit here alone for awhile.

(They start to leave, but he stops them)

Oh, wait a minute. Have you seen my sons this morning?

Lyla: Yes, we saw both of them, and they were arguing, as usual.

Father: What were they arguing about this time?

Jenny: Well, you know Mr. Elam likes to tease all the time.

Lyla: And he's lazy as all get out!

Father: I guess he wasn't helping with the chores again.

Lyla: Didn't look like it to me. He just stands around and pokes fun at the servants and his brother.

Jenny: I think sometimes Mr. Amos would like to punch him out, but he just walks away.

Father: I'll speak to him tonight.

(He walks over to the chair and sits down. Lyla and Jenny start toward the door)

Lyla: Huh! If you ask me, you need to do more than just speak to him.

(Father sits for awhile, shuffling restlessly. It"s obvious he is troubled by the report of his sons. He gets up and slowly leave the room, Momentarily, the two male servants, Jason and Jude enter)

Jason: The old man is not here.

Jude: Maybe we can ask him another time. I'm sure he will give us one of the heifers so we can celebrate when our cousin comes.

Jason: Especially since we have not seen our cousin in ten years.

Jude: I'm glad you didn't open your big mouth while that crazy Elam was in the shed. He would have spoiled everything.

(Father returns, followed by Elam who bounces around with his hands in his pockets. Jason and Jude leave hurriedly)

Father: Well, here you are, Son. I was just getting ready to send for you. We need to have a little talk. *(He sits down)*

Elam: Cool, Dad! Minds of great men run together. I need to have a little chat with you, too.

Father: Okay. What is it you wish to talk about?

Elam: Well, Dad, I need some cash. It's time I split from this shed. This place is squeezing my brain. I'm a big boy now!

Father: *(Stands up, startled)* What? What makes you think you deserve any money? I'm hearing that you are not doing your share of the work around here!

Elam: Whoa, who told you that? I work my tail off every day. I'll bet Amos is telling you this crap.

Father: I didn't say that. I want to be fair to both of you, but I would hope that you brothers would get along better.

Elam: Oh, so my brother Amos is the goodie, goodie dude who deserves everything, even your praise. I always knew you were partial to him.

Father: Can I not persuade you, my son? Look! My hands are shaking and my hair is white. I am old and I need the help of both my sons.

Elam: *(Raising his hands and shrugging his shoulders)* Okay. If my father does not feel I deserve anything, then I will go without it. I can make it on my own!

Father: Wait! Let me call Amos. We will make some decisions together. *(Father goes to the door and calls)* Amos! Come in here.

Amos: I heard all this babble about money. How dare you talk to Father like this?

Elam: Ah ha! So you were eavesdropping out there! Well let me tell you, Brother, you just get off my back You can have this rundown, rat-infested hole when the old man dies. I don't need any of you.

(He starts toward the door)

Father: Wait, Son. I can't let you leave without money. Life is hard enough when you have it. Here take this. *(He hands a bag to Elam and holds another for Amos)* I had already put this aside for your inheritance.

Amos: What is the meaning of this, Father. We don't need this as long as you are here with us. Let him go if he wants to! Elam, you should be ashamed to take it. When that runs out, don't come running back for more!

Elam: Don't worry, Brother. Maybe this life of digging in dirt and herding stinky sheep is for you, but there are greater things in store for me. Goodbye!

(He stuffed the bag under his arm and happily left the room)

Amos: Maybe this is good riddance, Father. He won't be missed that much. Especially when it comes to working.

(Father and Amos walk slowly out)

CURTAINS

Scene 2: Curtains open and Father is sitting in a chair on the porch; at times looking up, and then lowers his head in his hands. Amos, Jason and Jude enter and stands close to the entrance.

Amos: My heart goes out to my father. He is constantly watching for that no good Elam to return.

Jason: It's been more than a year since he left, and he has not heard from him. He should try to forget about him.

Jude: Some travelers came by yesterday. They talked about a famine in the land to the east. I hope Mr. Elam didn't get caught in it.

Amos: Yes. I heard it is causing all kinds of problems for the people. We are blessed that our flock and the land are still in good shape.

Jason: They say there are many deaths from starvation and sickness, and the land is drying up because there has been no rain.

Amos: I wonder about my brother. I venture to say that if his money is gone, so are his friends.

Jude: He would have to be in real bad shape before he would return.

Jason: But for your father's sake, I wish he would not tarry much longer.

Amos: My father's health is failing fast. He is suffering mostly because of Elam. I don't think he can hold out much longer.

Jude: If the young master does return, your father's health would improve very fast, believe me.

(Jude and Jason leave. Amos walks over and places his hands on his father's shoulders)

Amos: Father, I hate to see you sitting here day after day like this.

Father: My heart aches for my youngest son. I know him. He will spend and spend until all his money is gone. I pray he is not caught up in the problems people are having in the east.

Amos: If he's gotten himself into trouble, it's his fault. But he is clever enough to get himself out, even if he has to steal. Can I get something for you?

Father: Yes. Ask your mother to bring me a cool glass of water.

(Amos leaves, and shortly Mother comes in with a glass of water)

Mother: It's hot out here. Why don't you come inside?

Father: I'm fine. I want to watch the travelers go by. Maybe someone will stop and talk. Maybe someone has seen our son.

Mother: Here come some people now. They should be able to tell us just how bad it is over there.

(Two travelers, a man and a woman approach)

Traveler: Good evening, my good man. May we sit and rest a spell? My wife and I need a break.

Father: Yes. Come on up, I will get some chairs for you.

Traveler: No chairs. This will be fine. *(They sit on the steps)*

Mother: I'll get you a cool drink. I'm sure you must be tired from walking.

Wife: That would be fine. My husband and I have been walking for a long time, and the heat is sometimes unbearable.

Father: I take it you have come from the east. How bad is it there?

Traveler: I've never seen anything like this; like the days of the

Prophet Elijah. The sun smites like swords of fire, and the whole earth is burning in anguish.

Wife: I'm just thankful we got out in time. The trees have no leaves for shade. And the grass for cattle is all dried up.

(Mother brings a pitcher of water and two glasses)

Traveler: Thank you. People are dying of thirst, starvation, and the heat. Unless there is some relief soon, I'm afraid that area will be completely wiped out!

Wife: We are praying for rain, and I know the Lord will answer our prayers.

Father: My youngest son left home more than a year ago, and I have not heard from him. Maybe you have seen him. He is as fair as the morning, as generous as the river, and as cheerful as the birds in the air. You could recognize him a mile away.

Traveler: I'm sure we have not seen him. The only people we saw were tattered and begging. I'm sure your son was not among them.

Wife: Just to give you some idea how bad things are, we saw a young man who was so hungry, he hired himself to a swine farmer. As he fed the swine, he also ate with them.

Traveler: People are leaving in all directions. But from the devastation we saw, some will never get out alive.

Wife: I'm sure your son will return any day now. We will pray for him.

Father: I hope you're right. And thanks for your prayers.

Traveler: Thank you for the drink and a time for rest. We shall be going now.

Mother: And may God go with you. *(They wave goodbye)*

Father: My heart aches for my son. I can't help thinking he might be somewhere suffering.

Mother: *(Puts her hands on his shoulders)* Now don't you fret. Elam chose his path and only God knows and can help him. Why don't you come inside? It's hot out here.

Father: No. I think I'll just sit here a little longer.

(Mother leaves. He bows his head and the stage darkens)

Scene 3: While the stage is still darkened and Father is still seated on the porch distant sounds are heard. Spotlight catches the offstage scene.

Elam: *(Staggers along, stumbling and falling)*

Oh, mercy! Mercy Lord! ...
I'm so hungry. My friends all left me ... there's no one.

I've been such a fool. An idiot! Look at me, just a slob ...
Oh, why did I leave my father's house? He was such a good father ... the best father a son could ever have!
Oh mercy, mercy, mercy, Lord. Please help ...Please
My father's servants have bread to spare, and here I am so hungry!
I ate with pigs! I wallowed in the mud with pigs trying to get something to eat.
Oh help me, Lord. I don't believe I can make it!

(He climbs on a log and sits for a moment)

My family ... What would my family say?
I will go back; I will arise and go back to my father. I'll say to him: Father, please forgive me. I have treated you wrong ... I have sinned before God. Please just make me a servant and I'll be happy. Just don't turn me away. Father ...

(Lights go up on stage. Father raises his head as he hears the noise)

Father: What is that I hear? Elam! Elam! Is that you? *(He stands up and walks across the porch)* Elam! Elam! Is that you?

Mother: *(Rushes out when she hears him calling)* What's wrong with you, man! Sometimes I wonder if you will lose your mind worrying about that no-good son of ours.

Father: Hush, woman! Elam, is that you?

(By now Elam is crawling on his hands and knees)

Elam: Yes ... Yes ...Father, I'm here. Please help me!

(Father rushes off to help him. Mother is outraged)

Mother: Just look at you! Dirty, filthy, and smelling like a pig's pen!

Elam: I know. Father would you ... *(He reaches for a chair)*

Mother: Get off that chair! *(She screams)* Take your smelly hands off. How dare you come back here looking and smelling like an animal!

Father: Stop yelling, Woman. Let's hear what Elam has to say.

Elam: *(Kneeling on the floor in front of his father)* Father, I have sinned against heaven and before thee. I am not worthy to be called your son!

Mother: You're right about that! I am ashamed of you. Just wait until your brother sees you. *(She rushes to the door and calls Amos)* Amos, get in here!

Elam: Father, I did everything wrong. I was rotten. I lived and ate with the pigs. I know I don't deserve your mercy, but please don't send me away. Just make me one of your servants.

(Amos enters)

Amos: Phew! What is this?

Mother: It's your brother. Can you believe this?

Amos: Well, is this the way the prodigal returns home? Why are you on your knees, brother? Are you begging, or are you too hungry to stand up?

Father: Your brother is asking for forgiveness, Amos.

Amos: Ha! So this is the big man who was going away to make it on his own. What happened, brother? Someone took your cash while you were sleeping?

Father: That's enough, Amos. My prayers have been answered. My cup runneth over. My son was lost, but now he is home. Call the servants. *(He raised his arms in praise, then helps Elam to a chair)*

(Lyla, Jenny, Jason and Jude enter)

Jenny: Welcome home, master Elam!

Lyla: Yuk! Master who? *(She walks around holding her nose)*

Father: Jason, Jude, take my son, clean him up and dress him in the finest robe. Put a ring on his finger and shoes on his feet.

Amos: What?

Father: Then bring the fatted calf, kill and roast it. Let's eat and be merry, for this my son was dead, and is now alive again. He was lost but how he is found.

(Jason and Jude help Elam up and out the door)

Amos: My father rejoices for the one who left him. But I remained. I will not rejoice at the homecoming of a scoundrel!

Father: My son, you are ever with me, and all that I have is thine. Please do not fret. *(He reaches out for Amos, but Amos moves away)*

Amos: My father's hair is white and his shoulders are bent because of this prodigal. Of all the things I have done these many years, and you have never killed the fatted calf and celebrated with me. I will not rejoice!

Father: But isn't it fair that we should rejoice when one who was dead has come back to life again? He was lost and now he is found. Your brother has repented. God will forgive him, and so will we.

(Father puts his arm around Amos' shoulder and they leave)

CURTAINS

Scene 4: Jenny and Lyla are busy setting the table, bringing trays of food and pitchers of cool drinks for the feast. They place eight chairs around the table.

Jenny: Lyla, what do you make of all this?

Lyla: Huh! A banquet for a "bum". I don't believe it.

(Father enters and observes approvingly)

Father: This is very good!

(Jason and Jude enter followed by Elam who is magnificently dressed)

Father: Well, there you are, my son. And you look much better than you did the last time I saw you.

(The servants all laugh. Mother enters, and they begin seating themselves around the table)

Mother: Where is Amos?

Jude: I'll get him.

Lyla: He's probably still pouting.

Mother: Hush, girl!

(Amos enters slowly followed by Jude. He looks around in disgust, then finds a seat near the end of the table)

Father: Let us pray ...

(The little child is at the door jumping up and down, waving his arms trying to get attention. He has his brother and little sister with him)

Child: Hello, hello! Please, can we have something to eat?

(Father goes over and takes him by the hand. Jason and Jude places three more chairs at the table. The three scramble up quickly)

Father: Now, let us pray. Father, we bow to give thanks to you, not only for the food we are about to eat to nourish our bodies, but we give thanks to you for answered prayers. My son was lost, but now he is found. We can't thank you enough for these blessings, and we give you all the praises and honor. Amen.

Let's eat!

THE END

Friend

Synopsis

Marvin, a good student in high school is caught up in the net of peer pressure and dragging his feet in school. He finally meets FRIEND at summer camp and their association gradually nurtures Marvin back on the road to success.

Friend

CHARACTERS

Marvin, a high school junior who has been on and off the honor roll since 6th grade. He is an only son living with his mother while his father is away on a business trip.

Marvin's Mother, a kind and gentle woman who obviously loves her son and is very protective and encouraging.

Friend is a supernatural character, odd in appearance and seem to hang around Marvin like a guardian angel.

Mrs. Mayberry, a strict teacher who controls her classroom, and is dedicated to making scholars of all her students.

Mr. Walton and Mr. Kronk are recruiters from industry who visit high schools to offer scholarships and assistance to students who show exceptional aptitude in Math and Science.

Students

Calvin
Crickett
Janice
Jerry
Jim
Johnny
Pamela
Ray

Friend

Scene I: *The Carter's living room: Marvin is slouched on a chair almost hidden from view. He has a book in his hand, but watching TV. His mother enters carrying a knitting basket. She sits down and begins knitting. Suddenly she sees Marvin.*

Mother: Oh, Marvin I didn't know you were there! I thought you were going to the library today.

Marvin: Oh, no. I found a book in the library at school.

Mother: Did you bring it home?

Marvin: Well, no. I, uh, uh, I did the assignment at school.

Mother: Marvin, I've noticed you haven't brought home any books to study since school started, and you're in the third week now. What's going on?

Marvin: Oh, Mom! Everything is okay. We just haven't had many tough assignments yet. Most of the work I can finish during class time.

Mother: That's great. I just want you to get off to a good start this semester. You did a fantastic job with the community youth group this summer. Don't you think so?

Marvin: Oh, yeah. That was great.

Mother: Your new friend you met at camp, does he attend Washington High with you?

Marvin: No. Uh, no. I met him ... I mean, he goes to another school.

Mother: I see. You never mentioned his name. What is his name, Dear?

Marvin: Uh ... his name is, uh, Gabriel.

Mother: That's a nice name. I hope you will keep in touch with him. You seemed so excited to have him as a friend.

Marvin: Yea... yeah. He is.

(The phone rings)

Marvin: *(Gets up quickly)* I'll get it, Mom. Hello! Oh, hey Harry. When? How long will you be ... Just a minute, let me ask my mom. Mom, Harry asked me to go with him and his dad to the sporting goods store. Is that okay?

Mother: Yes, Dear.

Marvin: Okay, Harry. I'll be waiting outside. *(He hangs up the phone)* Thanks, Mom. I need to get out of the house and get some fresh air.

(Mother leaves. Marvin breathes a sigh of relief, picks up his jacket and starts for the door. Friend enters quietly)

Friend: Ah ha! So you didn't tell your mom all about me!

Marvin: *(Looking around nervously)* Oh, it's you! Well I didn't think Mom would understand.

Friend: Gabriel! I kinda like that name.

Marvin: How did you find me? I don't remember giving you my address.

Friend: Well, some things I already know.

Marvin: But, when we were at camp, you asked me for my address and my phone number, and ...

Friend: Just testing.

Marvin: How long are you going to be in town?

Friend: As long as you need me!

Marvin: But I'm doing okay, now. I was just a little depressed early in the summer. You know, leaving my friends and all.

Friend: As I recall, you also had some problems with being bored at home. And before your mom came in today, you were watching a nonsense story on that TV box over there, pretending you were reading.

Marvin: I was just relaxing for awhile. I was just tired from school and all.

Friend: Why did you tell your mom you didn't have homework?

Marvin: *(Startled)* You've been spying on me again. Were you looking through the window?

(Friend waits for an answer)

Marvin: Okay, Okay! I did kinda bend the truth a little, but I meant no harm. The homework is easy. I can do it before I go to bed tonight.

Friend: What kind of grades are you planning to get this term?

Marvin: Ohhhh! I'm going to bring back my honor status. You remember our conversation about setting goals? Well, I plan to be the best Engineer in the country one day. You just wait and see!

Friend: Good. That will require a lot of study.

Marvin I know.

Friend: You'd better go now. Harry and his father are outside waiting for you.

Marvin: *(Surprised)* How did you know ... Never mind. I'll see you. And thanks! You are going to leave before my mom comes back, aren't you?

Friend: No problem.

(Marvin leaves, and Friend leaves in the opposite direction)

CURTAINS

Scene 2: *Marvin, Jerry, Jim, Janice, Cricket, Johnny, Pamela, and Ray are seated on park benches talking.*

Janice: Marvin, you rushed off after school today. I thought we were going to walk home together.

Marvin: I'm sorry, Janice. I suddenly remembered my mom needed me at home right away.

Jerry: While we are all together, why don't we go over to the library and do that homework?

Jim: I'd rather get a good softball game going!

Johnny: Me too. But if I can get some help before I see that old batty teacher again, I'm all for it. Let's go to the library.

Pamela: Good idea. With all of us working, we'll have it done in no time.

Jim: Then maybe we can get the game going?

Crickett: Okay by me! I'll run over to my house and get some supplies.

(Crickett leaves. They all start off behind her but Marvin goes in the opposite direction)

Janice: Come on, Marvin. We need all the help we can get!

Marvin: I can't go. You guys go on. I'll just struggle through the assignment tonight.

Johnny: What's up, Marvin?

Jerry: Yeah! You seem to be moving out of the group. We haven't seen much of you since summer vacation. What's going on?

Pamela: For real! What's the deal? You don't want to be friends anymore?

Marvin: It's not that. You know we will always be friends. It's just that I have to help my mom around the house more while my dad is away. I'll be with you as soon as he gets home.

Ray: Well, if you get done in time, will you come on over?

Marvin: Sure will. See you later.

(Marvin leaves and Crickett returns with a bag of books and supplies)

Crickett: Here we are! I have the assignment sheets. We can make copies at the library. Hey, where is Marvin?

Jim: He had to leave.

Pamela: Hey, you guys! I don't mean to gossip about Marvin while he's not here, but he is really acting like a weirdo now!

Crickett: Is he ever! I saw him one day at summer camp and he was talking to himself.

Johnny: Aw, Crickett. Don't exaggerate.

Crickett: I'm not exaggerating. He was acting like he was really talking with someone. I looked, but I did not see a soul with him.

Ray: Crickett, you make the guy sound like a real "looney" now!

Janice: You certainly are, and I'm not sure that's fair since he's not here to defend himself.

Pamela: You know what I thought was odd? Marvin knew all the answers to the History questions in Mrs. Bragg's class yesterday. You know how he hates History.

Calvin: What startles me is how the overnight genius seems to be breezing through all the class discussions now. That's not the Marvin I know.

Jim: And he never seems to be bogged down like the rest of us.

Jerry: You're right! He does seem to be doing better than he did before.

Johnny: Oh, leave the guy alone. Maybe he has decided to get it together now. He is doing better than last year. How many of us can say the same?

Janice: I think I'll ask my mom if I can go over and study Trig with him tonight.

Calvin: Study? Yeah, right!

Crickett: Okay. Maybe you can find out what gives with our friend.

Johnny Seems to me, Janice, you would ask Marvin first. Maybe he doesn't want you to come over.

Jim: Really! The guy seems to be turning on the private act.

Pamela: Why don't you wait until he asks you to come over and study?

Janice: Okay, Pamela. Would you rather check him our? I notice you try to get the seat next to him in every class.

Pamela: I'm just being friendly, Janice. And furthermore, if you wouldn't be tardy to every class, maybe you could have the choice seat.

Crickett: Okay, girls! Let's knock it off.

Pamela: Don't worry, Janice. I don't plan to rain on your parade.

Janice: Thanks!

Jerry: Let's go, or we will soon be in the midst of a battle between the Marvin admirers.

(They leave. Marvin wanders back into the park with a book. He sits on the bench and begins flipping the pages. He finally puts the book down and cups his chin in his hands. Friend comes up quietly)

Friend: All done studying, Marvin?

Marvin: *(Startled)* Oh! No, I can't seem to concentrate. This stuff is difficult.

Friend: Maybe the park bench isn't the right place to study today.

Marvin: I guess.

Friend: I recall you couldn't concentrate on your prayers last night either. You were sitting up in bed.

Marvin: I know.

Friend: Why didn't you go the library with your friends today? Group study is sometimes a good idea.

Marvin: Well, I don't know.

Friend: Could it be you are afraid I will come with you?

Marvin: Well, I don't know. You were with me once at camp, and the others didn't seem to notice, but ...

Friend: I am <u>your</u> friend, Marvin. I would never embarrass you. Don't ever be ashamed of my presence.

Marvin: I'm not ashamed. It's just that ... well, I don't think they would understand.

Friend: I won't interfere.

Marvin: Were you in my History class yesterday?

Friend: Why do you ask?

Marvin: Well, even though I read the chapter, I wasn't sure I knew some of the answers and ...

Friend: Go on!

Marvin: But when I began talking, the answers suddenly seemed to come out right.

Friend: But you did not read the full chapter, Marvin.

Marvin: I know.

Friend: Why did you stop reading on page 71?

Marvin: I got tired. Well, no. I wanted to see a TV show. Well ...?

Friend: Procrastination does not pay off, you know. You might have known the answers to the final two questions if you had finished the chapter.

Marvin: I know.

Friend: I bet your friends could help you concentrate now at the library, and I am sure you could help with some of the problems.

Marvin: Okay. I'll try it. *(He hesitates)* But where will you be?

Friend: Around. Don't worry. I won't interfere or embarrass you.

Marvin: Thanks. And I won't forget to change my position for my prayers tonight.

(They leave in opposite directions)

CURTAINS

Scene 4: *Mrs. Mayberry's classroom. Students are milling around talking in small groups)*

Calvin: Hey, you guys! I got a radio. Let's have a dance party. Mrs. Mayberry doesn't seem to be coming today.

Crickett: Okay! Let's hear the music!

(Calvin turns the music on and they begin to dance while other stood aside and clapped. After a few minutes, Mrs. Mayberry comes in)

Mayberry: Here! Here! What do you think you are doing?

(They all race for their seats)

I am a few minutes late because of a traffic accident,

and you can't sit quietly and wait for me! Who has the radio? Calvin, come to my desk!

Calvin: Okay. It's my radio. But I only brought it because I didn't have time to go to my locker. I didn't want to be late for your class.

Mayberry: Just leave the radio on my desk, Calvin, and sit down.

(They all laugh)

Ray, I believe you owe me yesterday's homework assignment. Would you bring it to me now?

Ray: Uh, Mrs. Mayberry, I didn't complete the homework because Edison turned off our lights last night, and we all had to go to bed early.

Jim: What happened, Ray? Your old man blew his check again?

(They all laugh and Ray gets up and grabs Jim)

Mayberry: That's enough, Ray. Jim, if you can't hold your corny jokes, you will be here with me after school.

Before we get into today's lesson, I want to remind you that your best behavior is required today. Remember I told you last week that we would have visitors from the Grayport Engineering Corporation? Well, they should be here any minute now.

Pamela: Okay, guys. Get out your notes.

Mayberry: Yes, Pamela, you may use your notes today. I'm happy to know you are reading, listening, and taking notes.

Jerry: Mr. Mayberry, are these people looking for candidates to work in their company?

Mayberry: Who knows, Jerry. There could be scholarships for higher education if they see potential. So put on your thinking caps.

Janice: That's great! You see, guys, studying at the library just might pay off.

Mayberry: Oh, so you studied together yesterday. That sounds promising, but we have lost a lot of time today, and we might not get into that part of the lesson. But you will be okay in review.

(The two visitors come in and sit in back of the class. Mrs. Mayberry acknowledges their presence with a nod and continued)

Alright. Who can give me a good working definition of Trigonometry?

(They all look at each other blankly. Marvin stands up)

Marvin: It is a branch of Mathematics that deals with relations between angles in a triangle. *(He sits down)*

Mayberry: Good. But what are the processes?

(Silence again. Marvin stands up)

Marvin: There are functions and relations that determine the measurements.

Mayberry: Okay, class. Marvin has not been elected spokesman for the rest of you. Who remembers the names of these functions?

(Silence again)

Marvin, do you know?

Marvin: *(Stands)* I believe they are sine, cosine, secant, and tangent.

Mayberry: Thank you, Marvin. Now if I could get someone to tell us how Trigonometry measures angles, we can close this review.

(They all look at Marvin)

Marvin: The measurement of an angle corresponds to the amount of rotation required to move a line from the position of one of the lines to the other.

(The class applauds)

Mayberry: Great. Class, hold on to those notes you prepared for me today. We will do that lesson tomorrow. Now, let me introduce our guest. Mr. Walton and Mr. Kronk are from the Grayport Engineering Corporation. Gentlemen, meet the llth grade Trig class.

(The class applaud)

Walton: Thank you, Mrs. Mayberry for allowing us to visit today. This has certainly been a pleasure.

Kronk: Quite frankly, we have visited three other schools in the area and your class, at this time, is much more advanced. I believe your students will be right on target in preparation for the Engineering Search Test.

Walton. Yes. Early exposure and progress are very important. Within the next few weeks, your students should have covered vital portions in the testing area.

Kronk: Let me take this opportunity to congratulate all of you for hanging on to college preparatory courses.

Mayberry: Thanks to both of you. We were more than happy to have you. Please come again.

(The bell rings and students gather their books to leave. Kronk and Walton walk over to talk with Mrs. Mayberry. Marvin is the

last to leave the room. As he passes, the men reach out to shake his hand)

Walton: Congratulations, young man. You seem to be on your way to a career in Engineering.

Marvin: Yes sir!

Kronk: Don't forget to take the NEAS test when it is scheduled.

Walton: We will want to talk with you again after the test results are in.

Marvin: Yes, sir! Thank you. Thank you very much!

Mayberry: Marvin, ask your Gym teacher to phone me and I will excuse your tardiness to class.

(Mayberry and the two men leave the room. Marvin pumps his fist into the air excitedly)

Marvin: Yes! Yes!

(Friend moves quietly into the room)

Friend: How do you feel, Marvin?

Marvin: *(Waving his hands in the air)* How do I feel? Like I'm flying through the air and floating on clouds!

Friend: I guess you are excited.

Marvin: That is an understatement. You should have been here ...

Friend: I hope you noticed all the good things that happened today, and you will take time to figure out why they happened.

Marvin: Well, I know I have to thank you for all of this.

Friend: I just got here. But I can read your excitement.

Marvin: But how ... You mean ... I don't believe ...

Friend: Believe it, Marvin. I watched you study last night. You were seriously getting into it, as I knew you could.

Marvin: I studied until midnight. Not once did ... I mean, I didn't know you were there.

Friend: You missed your favorite TV show.

Marvin: I forgot about that, too.

Friend: That's good. You see now what you can do if you just concentrate on what is important.

Marvin: You bet. But I know you helped. You always do. You can't fool me.

Friend: I did listen to your prays last night.

Marvin: My prayers? Oh, yes. O yes ... Is this what you meant at camp last summer when you said, "If you have faith, and believe, and work, ask what you will, and ... Oh, God! Thank you!

Wow! Wow!

(Marvin was jumping and turning around in circles. When he stopped Friend had disappeared. He picked up his books and bounced out of the room)

THE END

Programs

for

Special Occasions

The First Noel

A Christmas Pageant

Based on the Bible Story that is never told too often,
The Magnificent Birth of Jesus
from
The Gospels of Matthew, Mark, and Luke
New King James Version
The Holy Bible

The First Noel

Needed for presentation

Choirs: Youth and Children's *(Candles for each)*
Soloist: Sweet Little Jesus Boy
Narrators (at least 6)
Shepherds (unlimited number; costumes: head dress, robes, and staffs)
One Angel (creative costume)
Innkeeper in costume
Many children with wrapped gifts (costumes optional)
Drummer Boy (costume: brimmed cap, knickers with suspenders, brightly colored shirt, drum and drum sticks
Mary and Joseph in costume
Anna, a prophetess in costume
Simeon, a man from Jerusalem, in costume

SONGS:
Silent night
O Little Town of Bethlehem
Away in a Manger
Sweet Little Jesus Boy
Alleluia
Joy to the World
Rise Up Shepherd and Follow
Glory to God
We Three Kings
Drummer Boy
O Come All Ye Faithful

All songs except "Drummer Boy" and "Glory to God" are found in the National Baptist Hymnal. Glory to God may be improvised. The words are important.

Narrator for "Silent Night" should be very dramatic.

Scene 1

Manger in center front – elevated
Babe in swaddling cloth
Stool for Mary to sit on – Joseph kneels

Large pictures or figures of animal for real life effect, and straw around the manger

Star above the manger (electrical)

****

Upon entering, Youth and Children's choirs
will sit in the choir stand

Narrators will use microphones on both side of stage alternating as they speak

Scene 2

Children who enter will sit on steps at left and right of Manger. If more seating is needed, they should sit on front pews.

Lights are dim except the podium lights and the spotlight on the Manger when Joseph and Mary are in place. Soft music (Silent Night) plays as first Narrator recites slowly, following the music.

It is a Silent Night... A Holy Night... All is quiet, and the stars are shining brightly ... There she is, the Virgin Mother and her child ... He is a Holy infant, so tender and so mild ... sleeping so peacefully... A Heavenly peace.

Tonight ... the shepherds are amazed at the brightness of the stars in the heavens ... And there is the sound of the Heavenly Host singing Alleluia ... Alleluia ... For Christ the Saviour is born.

Yes ... the Son of God is born ... and radiance beams from His Holy face ... This is the dawn of redeeming grace for us all ... This is Jesus ... Lord at His birth ... This is Emmanuel.

Choirs process with lighted candles singing the first verse of Silent Night. They move up the to choir loft from both sides so they will be separated. Candles are blown out all together before they are seated. The spotlight follows the choirs. Mary and Joseph leave carrying the baby during the procession.

Narrator 1: Good evening! Tonight we shall take you back to Judea and the time when Herod was King; and to Jerusalem, and the birth of the Christ Child. Even though many prophecies had been written about the coming of the Messiah, Zacharies and his wife Elisabeth were given privileged information after learning they would become parents of John, the forerunner of Christ. The angel Gabriel appeared to Zacharies with the good news. It is no wonder that he and Elisabeth were surprised, for they had grown old and had no children.

Narrator 2: About a month later, the angel Gabriel was sent by God to Nazareth, to the village of Galilee. *(Gabriel enters left stage and meets Mary who enters from right stage)* He appeared to a virgin named Mary, who was engaged to become the wife of Joseph, a descendant of King David. Gabriel said unto Mary," Congratulations, fair lady. The Lord is with you, and will wonderfully bless you. Very soon now you will become pregnant and bear a son, whom you will call Jesus. He will be the Messiah". Mary was surprised, of course, for being a virgin and not yet married to Joseph was frightening. But the angel consoled her, "Don't be afraid, Mary. The Holy Spirit will come upon you, and the power of God will overshadow you. Six months ago, your aunt Elisabeth, the barren wife of Zacharies, was blessed by God to bear a son. Why not go and visit with her."

(Mary and Gabriel leave together)

Song: Alleluia (Verses 1 and 3)

Narrator 3: And so it was that Caesar Augustus, the Roman Emperor, decided that a census should be taken. Everyone was required to return to his ancestral home for this registration. So Joseph took his pregnant wife to Bethlehem in Judea. *(Joseph and Mary enter)* And while they were there, the time came for Mary's baby to be born. Together they wandered about town looking for a place to stay, but there was not one room. *(The innkeeper comes in and leads Joseph and Mary to the stable and the Manger)* Finally, an innkeeper led them to a lowly stable where she had her baby. Joseph carefully wrapped the baby in a warm blanket and laid him in the manger. There he slept peacefully.

Song: Away in a Manger (Children's choir sing all verses)
Solo: Sweet Little Jesus Boy

Narrator 4: That night some shepherds were in the fields outside the village, guarding their flock. Suddenly an angel appeared among them, and the landscape became as bright as day with the glory of the Lord. They were all frightened. The angel said, "Fear not, for I bring you tidings of great joy. In the quiet of the night, the Saviour, the promised Messiah is born in the city of Bethlehem. Go and see". They asked, "But how will we recognize Him?" The angel said, "You will find the baby wrapped in swaddling clothes and lying in a manger. Just follow the star to Bethlehem".

(Shepherds enter slowly from the back down the aisles while the Children's Choir sings)

Song: Rise up Shepherd and Follow - all verses (Children's choir)

Shepherds: (Recite the 23rd Psalm)
The Lord is my shepherd, I shall not want. He maketh me to lie down in green pastures; he leadeth me beside the still waters. He restoreth my soul. He leadeth me in paths of righteousness for His name's sake. Yea, though I walk through the valley of the shadow of death, I will fear no evil; for thou art with me; Thy rod and thy staff they comfort me. Thou prepareth the table before me in the presence of mine enemies. Thou anointest my head with oil; my cup runneth over. Surely goodness and mercy shall follow me all the days of my life; And I will dwell in the house of the Lord forever.

(They stand staring at the manger)

Narrator 5: Suddenly, the angels are joined by the heavenly host praising God and singing, "Glory to God in the Highest, peace on earth, goodwill to all men".

(Angel walks behind the manger and raises her wand)

Song: Glory to God in the Highest (Both Choirs) Melody optional.

Glory to God in the highest
Glory to God in the highest
And peace on earth,
Goodwill to all men.

(The angel and the shepherds leave as they had entered)

Narrator 5: The shepherds returned to the fields and told others what they had seen. And all who heard their story came to see the Christ Child. Many people were already on their way to pay their taxes and to register for the census. So they gathered their gifts and made their way to the place where the baby was born. They came from far and near, following the star of Bethlehem.

Song: Joy To The World (Verses 1 and 2)

(People come from all directions bringing gifts for the Christ Child. They placed the gifts around the Manger and sat down. All joined in the singing)

Narrator 5: The news spread rapidly through the countryside. It seemed the whole world was charged with excitement. For after all, the Prophet Isaiah had foretold the coming of Christ. And somehow, the mystery of who He would be was baffling to many, to say the least.

People: (Recite together) "For unto us a child is born, unto us a Son is given. And the government shall be upon his shoulder; and his name shall be called Wonderful, Counselor, The Mighty God, The Everlasting Father, The Prince of Peace."

Narrator 5: In the neighboring provinces, the Kings heard the news and hurried to see what the excitement was all about. They too, remembered the prophecy of Isaiah. "Therefore, the Lord himself shall give you a sign. Behold, a virgin shall conceive and bear a son, and shall call his name Emmanuel."

(Three Kings enter. They examine the child and place their gifts beside the Manger. They sing)

Song: We Three Kings Of Orient Are – Kings sing verse I, and choir joins in the refrain.

Narrator 6: What a birthday party! There was one little lad who came along and beat upon his drum. He too had heard of the birth of a King and wanted to praise Him in his own way.

Song: The Little Drummer Boy (All sing as the little boy enter beating his drum)

Narrator 6: When the time came for Mary's purification offering at the Temple, the parents took the baby to Jerusalem to present Him to the Lord. There was a prophetess named Anna, who was very old, came to see the baby. *(Anna enters slowly and walks over the see the baby)* She had never left the temple, but worshipped night and day, fasting and praying. She gave thanks to God by raising her arms, and spoke of the child to all who were there. And then she walked slowly away.

(Simeon enters)

Narrator 6: And then came a man called Simeon. He was a good man who, for many years waited for the Messiah to come. For the Holy Spirit had revealed to him that he would not die until he had seen the Messiah. He took the child from Mary's arms, raised him in the air and began praising God. "Lord, now I can die content. For I have seen Him as you promised. I have seen the Saviour you have given to the world. He is the Light that will shine upon all nations." Then he gave the child back to Mary and said, "A sword shall pierce your soul, for this Child shall be rejected by many. But he will be the greatest joy of us all. Let heaven and earth praise His Name.

(As Simeon leaves, pianist begin playing the finale: O Come All Ye Faithful. Narrator 6 motions to the choir and the audience to stand and join in the singing)

The End

Who Is This Man?

A simulated radio broadcast of the events in the life of Jesus Christ, beginning on Palm Sunday and culminating during occurrences surrounding the Resurrection

Who Is This Man?

Suggestions for production

If possible, there should be 4 stationary sets in different places for broadcasting:

1. For the director, a table, left or right stage, with a large radio, and a chair.

2. Three separate places for three reporters. No furniture is necessary.

3. Headphone for director, microphones for the reporters.

For an evening production, a spotlight is most effective as the program does not show action.

Canned sound tracts can be supplemented for actual crowd noise.

Biblical characters should be in costumes.

Who Is This Man

*

CHARACTERS

Director: Ted Wise

Reporters:
Susan Smith
Jim Matthews
Mary Ann West

Lazarus
Spokesman
Voice of Peter
Voices of the Crowd

Apostle
Guard
Mary of Galilee
John

Director: Good evening. Welcome to WWJD News. I am Director Ted Wise. We are coming to you live from Jerusalem. As you know, crowds are gathering here for the Feast of the Passover. But there's one person making news today. It is Jesus of Nazareth, whom many claim, is the Messiah. We have reporters stationed in many areas so that we may capture as much news as possible. For the latest report on this astounding miracle-worker, let's go to Susan Smith in Bethany. Susan!

(Spotlight moves to Susan and Lazarus)

Susan: This is Susan Smith in Bethany. I have been talking with Jesus' friend Lazarus. This is the Lazarus whom Jesus reportedly brought back from the dead. Lazarus, do you know what Jesus' plans are for today?

Lazarus: This morning word got around that He was going to the city for the Passover Feast, so we were all up at sunrise. He sent two of the fellas ahead to get a donkey. They are scheduled to meet Him in Bethphage. That's all I know.

Director: Susan, we have word that one or more of His disciples are already inside Jerusalem. Does Lazarus know if this is true?

Lazarus: Listen! No one knows what Jesus will do next. I believe Judas is in Jerusalem now to take care of some expenses before the Feast.

Susan: Thank you, Lazarus. *(Lazarus leaves)* I believe Jim Matthews is with someone from the Sanhedrin Council. Jim!

(Spotlight moves to Jim and the Spokesman)

Jim: Yes, Susan. We're here with a spokesman from the Council Sir, it seems that Jesus is coming directly into the city with a very large group of his followers. How do you react to this?

Spokesman: I can only say, we don't want any trouble here today! *(He leaves)*

Jim: Sorry, Susan. He just took off!

(Spotlight moves back to the Director)

Director: Let's bring in Mary Ann West who has been following the crowd more closely. Mary Ann!

(Spotlight moves to Mary Ann)

Mary Ann: This is Mary Ann West reporting from the gate. There is no question now; Jesus of Nazareth is making history. Everybody seems to know about Him because of his activities over the last few days.

Director: Mary Ann, we can hear noise in the background. What seems to be going on now?

(Crowd noise and horse's hooves gradually grow louder)

Mary Ann: Peter has been leading the crowd all day. They seem to be chanting something over and over. Wait! They are getting closer and we should be able to hear them clearly in a minute or two.

Peter: Rejoice greatly, O daughter of Zion! Shout loudly, O Jerusalem! Behold your King cometh! Hosanna to the son of David! Blessed is he that cometh in the name of the Lord!

Mary Ann: Jesus appeared just seconds ago riding on a donkey. People are breaking palm branches and spreading them on the road ahead of him. They are beginning to chant with Peter so you won't be able to hear me.

Peter: Behold your King! Hosanna! Hosanna!

Crowd: Hosanna! Hosanna! Blessed is He that cometh in the name of the Lord! Hosanna! Hosanna! Blessed be the name of the Lord!

(Spotlight goes out. A musical interlude drowns out the noise of the crowd. After this, the broadcast begins again with noise in the background. Spotlight flashes to the Director and then to Susan)

Director: Susan, are you still in Bethany? Come in, Susan!

Susan: No, Ted. I rushed back from Bethany because most of the people left town to join the procession to Jerusalem behind Jesus. There are no officials out here to stop Him, and I'm sure the noise can be heard all over the valley. I'm signing off now so I can move ahead of the crowd.

(Spotlight moves back to the Director)

Director: Again, this is station WWJD. In case you have just tuned in, there is a rumor that Jesus will be tried and sentenced to death today. The charges are not clear at the moment, but it sounds like treason. The word we have now, they have already found a place for the execution. Oh, no! This sounds like a crucifixion! We're signing off now until we can get more information. As soon as we can, we will bring you up to date.

(Spotlight goes out. Again music drown out the noise. This lasts for a longer period of time, and then the spotlight is on the Director)

Director: Good morning! This is Ted Wise again, reporting from WWJD radio station. While we were off the air, there has certainly been a turn of events as we were following the story of Jesus. Our reporter, Jim Matthews, has some news of last night's events. Jim!

(Spotlight changes to Jim)

Jim: Yes, Ted. Yesterday they seized Jesus and arrested Him. It is rumored that one of His closest friends turned Him over to the authorities. A trial was held during the night in quite an unusual manner. Pilate couldn't seem to find evidence of a crime to convict Jesus, or he didn't want to. But the crowd was persistent. So another prisoner by the name of Barrabas was released and Jesus was convicted. This is their custom, you know. There was no pity there. Only ridicule!

Director: Thanks, Jim. Susan, come in!

(The noise has changed now to yelling, weeping and wailing. Spotlight changes to Susan)

Susan: This is Susan Smith again. I am with the crowd of people now following Jesus up the hill. This scene has turned real ugly. The solders are lashing Jesus as He struggles with carrying a heavy cross. He seems to be very weak, bleeding and stumbling. Wait! Now they have pulled a man out of the crowd to help Him. The man next to me says he is Simon of Cyrene.

Director: Thank you, Susan. We have located one of Jesus' close friends at the bottom of the hill. Mary Ann is talking with him. Let's listen.

(Spotlight changes to Mary Ann and the man)

Mary Ann: Sir, I believe you know this man, Jesus. Tell me, what are your feelings about all of this?

Apostle: I don't know. I just don't know. I'm shocked, and I am ... I just didn't know this would happen. He talked about dying, but I can't believe it's going to happen. *(He leaves quickly)*

Mary Ann: Sorry, Ted. I don't think he wanted to talk anymore. He just ran away.

(Spotlight moves to Susan)

Susan: Well, Ted, there is no question what Jesus' fate is. This is a gruesome scene. Two thieves are already on crosses as Jesus is being lifted up, nailed to the cross and bleeding from his side, his hands, feet, and seemingly his whole body. He can be heard muttering something. I am not close enough to hear. But, there is a sound like the rumbling of an earthquake getting louder now. I just heard one of the soldiers say, "This truly must have been the Son of God". This scene is over, Ted. It's too dark out here to see.

(The earthquake is loud, but finally fades into music again as the spotlight goes out. After the interlude, the spotlight is on the Director while Jim speaks.

Jim: Ted, this is Jim. I don't know where you want to start with this, but I think I can get some reaction from one of the first women at the grave.

Director: Good. But first, I've got Susan who is speaking with one of the guards right now. I'll get back to you. Go ahead, Susan!

(Spotlight moves to Susan and the Guard)

Susan: Susan Smith here at the Roman garrison stationed at the tomb of Jesus. We must keep the guard's name secret. Sir, can you tell us what happened here?

Guard: Well, we were on guard here all night. At one

instance, we felt a tremble of the ground and we were shaken. But before we could contain ourselves, there was another vibration like a full scale earthquake. It was so sharp, I think I hit my head on something when I fell to the ground. I don't know how long I lay there but when I woke up, I was sure I saw a man in white flying out of the sky and landing on the tomb!

Susan: What did you do?

Guard: His appearance was like a bolt of lightning. I think we all fainted, and I believe we were out cold about 15 or 20 minutes. All I could think of when I came around and saw the empty tomb was, they really managed to pull this thing off. They had taken the body of Jesus.

Susan: You mean there was no one in the tomb?

Guard: Only the linens Jesus was wrapped in were lying on the slab. It looked as though he had disintegrated inside of them!

(Director interrupts, but spotlight goes over to Jim)

Director: Just a minute, Susan. We've been able to reach Jim with one of first women at the tomb after it was empty. She is a woman named Mary. Jim, are you there?

Jim: Yes, Ted. Mary, tell us what you know about this.

Mary: Well, on the Sabbath, we prepared the spices to anoint His body, but we did not take it to the grave until the next day. As we approached the grave, we could see that the stone had been rolled away. When I looked Inside, there was a man dressed in white sitting where Jesus' body should have been.

Jim: And then what happened?

Mary: When the man told us Jesus was not there, we came out. It was then I saw Him. At first I thought he was a gardener. But when He looked at me and called my name, I knew it was Jesus.

Jim: Ted, she was crying when I first started talking with her, but now she suddenly left, skipping and waving her hands.

(Spotlight moves to the Director)

Director: Thank you, Jim. As you can imagine, this story has taken on dimensions we had not anticipated. We have word that Jesus appeared to two of His followers as they were walking home. Mary Ann has that report. Mary Ann!

(Spotlight moves to Mary Ann)

Mary Ann: Yes, Ted. A moment ago I was with one of Jesus' followers. He reports that he and a friend were walking along the road to Emmaus when suddenly someone was walking beside them. They talked for awhile, and when He started quoting the scriptures to them, they knew it was Jesus. They persuaded Him to come home with them, and they ate a meal together.

(Spotlight changes to Susan and John, one of the disciples)

Susan: Ted, I have one of the disciples who broke bread with Him. Sir, who are you and what happened?

John: My name is John. We were together eating. Two people came barging in the room saying they had just been with Jesus.

Susan: How did you react?

John: We were startled and frightened at first. Then He

appeared in the room with us without opening a door or window, and asked, "Why are you troubled? See the nail prints in my hands and feet?" He invited us to touch Him and we just couldn't contain our joy. And so He broke bread with us and reminded us of His death and resurrection so that we would not have to suffer as He did. We are free at last. All we have to do now is go and tell others about Jesus and His love for all who believe in Him.

(Spotlight moves back to Director)

Director: Well, this story has been reported from many sources, and there is no doubt it will be reported again and again, for in the minds of these people, Jesus is the risen Lord. If anyone is still doubting and wondering what this will mean in the coming days, I guess only time will tell. But as for now, Jesus is risen!

THE END

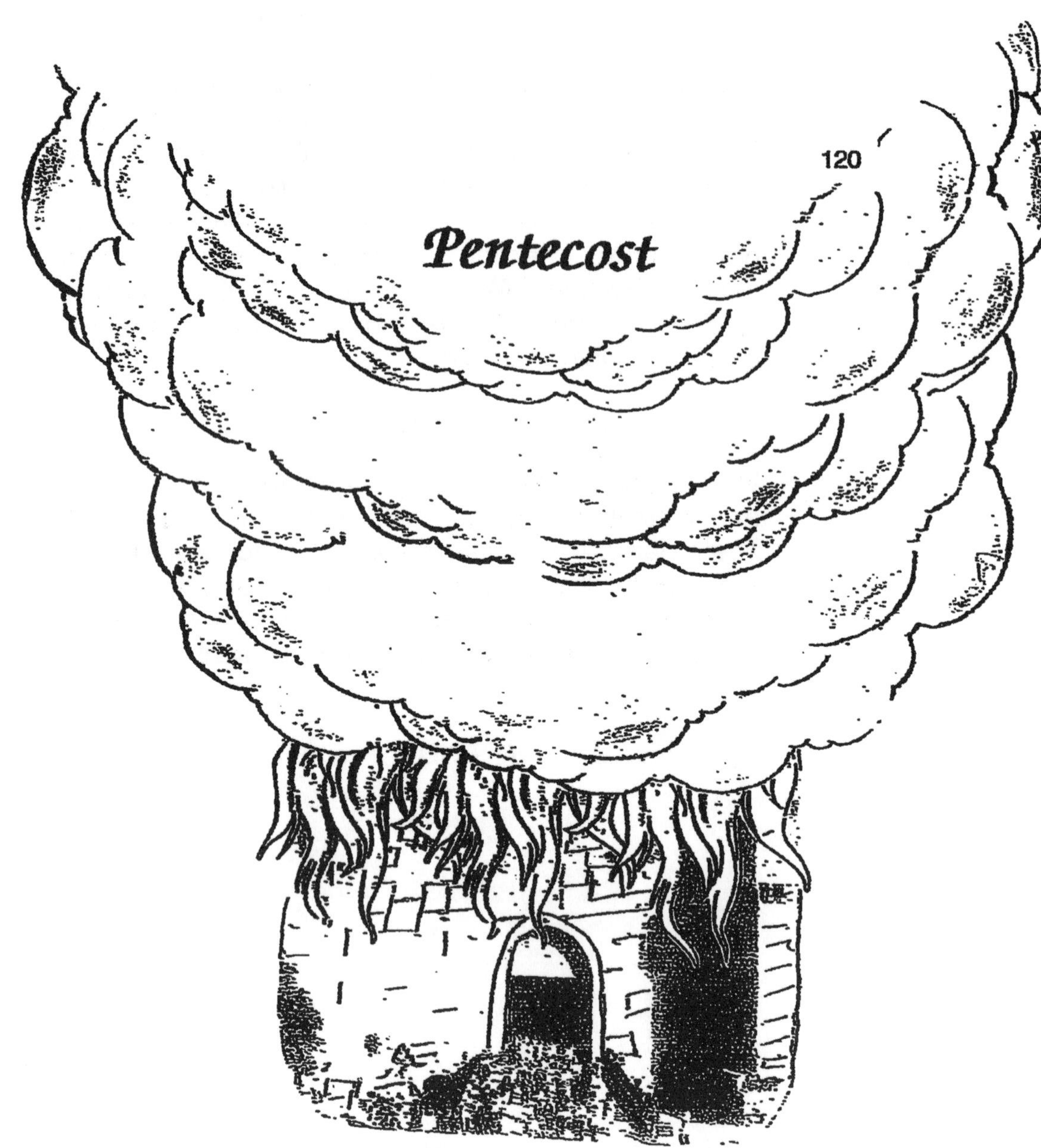

A Sunday School Presentation

Christians celebrate Pentecost annually on a designated Sunday, assuming that fifty days from Passover to the Feast of Weeks were counted until the day after the seventh sabbath (our Sunday) The Old Testament description is found in Leviticus 23:15-16.

According to research, there are some Christian churches that do not celebrate or acknowledge Jewish traditions. But many others revere and regard the heritage and doctrine of the Churches the apostles worked so hard to to establish.

The Spirit's timing for the launch of the Church could not have been better. The death and resurrection of Jesus Christ turned into the only true Spiritual Harvest.

Pentecost

A Sunday School Presentation

*

CHARACTERS

Eight Sunday School Students

Barbara	Joe
Bobby	Karen
Ernie	Mary
John	Susan

Mrs. Kay, Director of
Christian Education

Pentecost

Eight students are seated around a table waiting for the Sunday School Teacher to come in.

Karen: Our teacher is late today. I wonder if she is coming.

Barbara: I don't think we are having regular Sunday School today. Someone's supposed to come for a special program.

Joe: Yeah! That's why we are meeting here instead of our classroom.

Bobby: What's so special about today?

Susan: It's Pentecost Sunday.

Mary: Pentecost! What's Pentecost?

John: It's a special Sunday that comes after Easter.

Bobby: But what is it? What happened on Pentecost?

Ernie: I think it's when lots of people became Christians.

(Mrs. Kay enters with a folder in her hand. She hands a sheet of paper to each student)

Mrs. Kay: You are absolutely right, Ernie. And I brought some information along so that we might know more about the significance of the celebration of this day. Here, we will read some information that came from the Bible. It is simplified so we will understand it more fully. Each page has a number so we can follow the story. You may stop at any time and ask questions, if you wish.

Karen: Okay, I have number one. Shall I read?

Mrs. Kay: Yes, Karen.

Karen: The story of Pentecost is found in the second chapter of Acts. But the Prophet Joel speaking for the Lord centuries ago concerning no other God except Himself said, "And ... I will pour out my Spirit on all people. Your sons and daughters will prophesy, your old men will dream dreams, and your young men will see visions".

Barbara: I have number two. The prophesy came true. The Day of Pentecost came, and Jesus' disciples gathered together, and suddenly, a noise like a rushing wind came from Heaven. The noise filled the whole building.

Joe: Tongues of flames came down to rest on each disciple, and they began to speak all kinds of native languages, because each man was filled with the power of the Holy Spirit.

Mrs. Kay, does this mean only the disciples were treated with the tongues?

Mrs. Kay: Well, most of the scripture interpretations refer to the disciples, but as you will see, the crowd that had gathered for the annual festival were there and were certainly affected by this experience. Read on.

Bobby: Many Jews who lived in Jerusalem but originally came from other countries heard the disciples speaking in their native languages. They accused them of drinking too much wine. Peter raised his voice and shouted, "We have not been drinking wine! Who would drink wine this early in the morning"?

Mary: Peter continued, "You are forgetting what God said through the Prophet Joel. He said we would see wonders in the sky, signs on earth, and everyone who accepted Jesus would be saved.

Oh! So that's what He meant by pouring His Spirit on all men, and they would prophesy and see visions, and dream dreams, or something like that!

Mrs. Kay: That's correct. Read on, John.

John: The people gathered around the disciples and started whispering to each other, but Peter raised his voice and they stopped to listen. "Men of Israel, you have seen Jesus of Nazareth perform miracles and wonders. You know He was crucified, and that God raised Him from the dead because death had no power over Him".

Ernie: Peter continued: "David knew the Messiah would come some day. He said the Lord was always at his right hand. David was happy because he knew that through Christ, he would be saved and would go to Heaven. Never doubt that! The man you crucified, Jesus of Nazareth, is the Christ."

(They all put their papers down and applauded)

Karen: Listen to this! Peter told the people they should repent and be baptized in the name of Jesus Christ for the forgiveness of their sin. He said if they would do this, they would receive the gift of the Holy Spirit. Many people did believe him, and about three thousand were baptized that day.

Barbara: Wow! This sounds like the beginning of the Church. So celebrating Pentecost is kinda like celebrating the Church's birthday!

Mrs. Kay: Oh, yes. You see together all who were baptized and received the Holy Spirit formed a unified group of dedicated followers. God intended that all of them would be witnesses for Him.

Joe: Just like He wants all of us who have received His salvation to be witnesses for Him.

Susan: That really is the whole purpose of the church, isn't it?

Mrs. Kay: Absolutely!

Mary: Why can't we celebrate the birth of the Church now? This is awesome!

Mrs. Kay: I thought you'd never ask! Boys, go back there and bring out the cake. Let's ask the pastor to come in and blow out the candles.

(Mary ran out and came back with the pastor)

Pastor: Mary told me about your lesson today. I would be pleased to join you.

Mary: Now, let's sing.

Happy birthday to you;
Happy birthday to you;
Happy birthday dear Church,
Happy birthday to you.

THE END

The Lord's Prayer

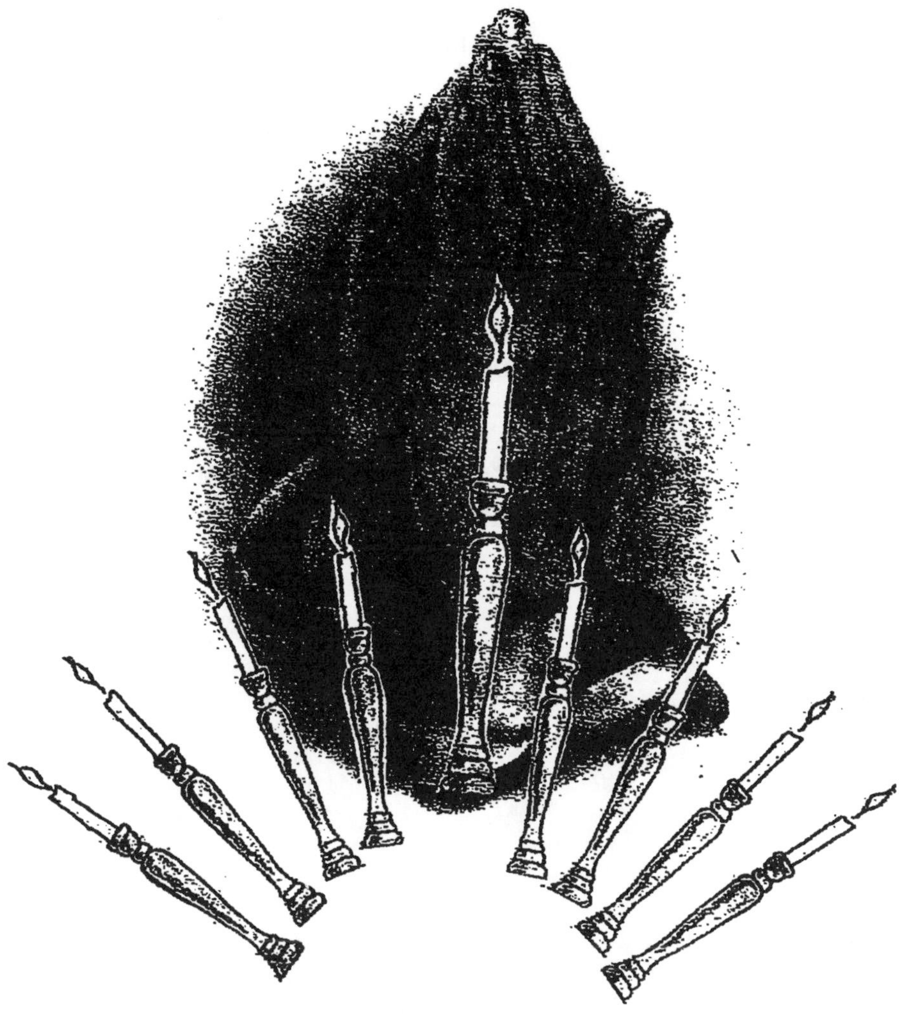

Symbolized With Candles in Narration and Song

The Lord's Prayer Symbolized With Candles

The original service was prepared and given by the Welsh Association at the Eastern Pennsylvania State Convention sometime ago.

This similar version has been written and performed with song. It was presented at the
Sarah Fisher Home for Children
in Southfield, Michigan
March, 1997
by the
Charles G. Adams Drama Group
Hartford Memorial Baptist Church

Variety ... Program, by Lois Kerns Brown; Copyright 1947; National Baptist Training Union Board, Nashville, Tennessee.

THE LORD'S PRAYER SYMBOLIZED WITH CANDLES

Soloist: Our Father, which art in Heaven; Hallowed be thy name ...

First Speaker lights the tall White Candle:

"Our Father" ... The tallest candle is white for purity, and it represents Our Father God. This prayer is for the Christian Community or the Christian family, with God being the head. Just as our earthly father takes care of us, we are a group bound together with ties of love as only God can love us. When Jesus was teaching this prayer to His apostles, He, no doubt, was teaching a pattern for believers to follow. And when it is used in a group, we are as one with followers of Christ; for God is our Father.

Second Speaker lights a Blue Candle:

"Our Father, who art in Heaven". I am lighting a blue candle which reminds us of the heavens above us. Through faith we know that God has prepared a better place for us. It is a heavenly place where we will rest from our labors here on earth, and we will be with Him. God is beyond the blue, and by His light, He is everywhere. From His throne in Heaven He is watching over us. Thanks be to God.

Third Speaker lights a Green Candle:

"Hallowed be Thy Name"... Now we light the green candle, for this is the everlasting color. We think of the great cedars and pine trees in all their splendor. The name of God is everlasting. The NAME sums up the whole person of God. So long as the earth shall stand, His name will be spoken with reverence and praise. In Ezekiel 36:23, God says, "I will honor my great name that you have defiled, and the people of the world shall know that I am Lord". This is the word of the Lord.

Soloist: Thy Kingdom come, Thy will be done on earth, as it is in Heaven...

Fourth Speaker lights a Purple Candle:

> "Thy Kingdom come" ... I am lighting a purple candle because purple is a royal color. Purple is a Kingdom color. Thy Kingdom come is the petition of all Christians to build up the Kingdom of God. We long for the day when God will overthrow the kingdom of this world; a world where satan walks boldly down the streets with no fear of God. We live for the day when the kingdom of this world will become the Kingdom of our Christ and will show in more and more people of this world. Whenever we let our light shine we are helping God to build His Kingdom. Praise be to God.

Fifth Speaker lights a Brown Candle:

> "Thy will be done on earth as it is in Heaven" ... I am lighting a brown candle to represent the earth. And remember the blue candle that is already burning represents Heaven. Here we link the kingdom of this world and the Kingdom that is to come. We are reminded that OUR will is not a priority, but God's will should be our guide. When we allow God's will to be done in our lives, we are living so others will see Christ in us.

Soloist: Give us this day, our daily bread. And forgive us our debts, as we forgive our debtors ...

Sixth Speaker lights a Yellow Candle:

> "Give us this day our daily bread" ... I am lighting a yellow candle that reminds us of the golden fields of grain waiting to be harvested. This prayer is for all our temporal needs, not luxuries. He taught that we should not be anxious about what we need to eat or to wear. For, just as He adorns the lilies of the fields and feed the birds of the air, He will

certainly take care of us. He teaches day by day our dependence upon Him. Thanks be to God!

Seventh Speaker lights a Silver Candle:

"Forgive us our debts as we forgive our debtors" ... For this, I light a silver candle to represent the coins with which we pay our bills. This is not an easy prayer. I show you the number 490. Did you know that it is contained in a commandment from Jesus? When one of the disciples asked how many times we should forgive another person, Jesus told him 70 times 7, which is 490. When we sin, we become debtors to God and maybe to someone else. And we must remember that God's forgiveness of us does not depend on whether or not we forgive others. It is by His grace that He does so. But how can we ask God's forgiveness when we are not willing to forgive others?

Soloist: "And lead us not into temptation; but deliver us from evil ...

Eighth Speaker lights a Red Candle:

"And lead us not into temptation" ... I am lighting a red candle because red stands for the blood shed for our sins. Temptation, if we yield to it, will surely lead to sin. Christians know their weakness and readiness to sin, so they must pray that they be strengthened to resist temptation. God does not tempt us, but we are tempted by our own evil desires. This is why we ask God to make us strong enough to resist temptation. And when we resist, we grow in grace. Thanks be to God.

Ninth Speaker lights a Black Candle:

"But deliver us from evil" ... I am lighting a black candle because evil is darkness. 1 John 1:5b says, "God is light; in Him there is no darkness." We live in a world where evil and sin are all around us. Alone, we cannot fight the forces of evil, mainly because we have thoughts and seeds of sin In our nature. These can become fertile with our everyday experiences. We need God's help to fight the forces of evil.

Tenth Speaker lights an Orange Candle:

"For Thine is the Kingdom, the Power and the Glory forever". Remember, the purple candle is still burning for the Kingdom. Now I light the orange candle to depict the Glory of God. Orange reminds us of a glorious sunset. It is like a magnificent picture painted by a famous artist in the sky, and God is that great artist. This doxology reminds us also of the sovereignty of God which will remain forever, and forever, Amen.

Soloist: Give us this day our daily bread. And forgive us our debts, as we forgive our debtors. And lead us not into temptation, but deliver us from evil. For Thine is the Kindgom, and the Power, and the Glory forever. Amen.

THE END

God's Hand in Black History

A Program presented by the
Sunday School Department at
Hartford Memorial Baptist Church
Detroit, Michigan
Sunday, February 16, 1999

Devotion:

Song: Lift Every Voice and Sing

Prayer: Senior High student #1

Scripture: Psalm 139:1-10 – Responsive Reading led by Senior High School student #2

Song: Just Look Where The Lord Has Brought Us. *(Sunday School Students)*

(Teachers have prepared their groups for various Black History presentation)

1. Introduction by Senior High student #3:

   Good morning. The title of our assembly today is "God's Hand in Black History". As we read our Bibles, and learn of the struggles throughout history, we do have a lot to be thankful for. We can see that our people in Old Testament times lost their even playing field among men early on, but not so with God. Junior High students will bring to us five brief biographies.

2. Junior High presentation … *(Examples are attached)*

3. Narration by Senior High student #4:

   The Civil Rights movement during the time of Dr. Martin Luther King, Jr. made an indelible impression upon the world; even upon the little children. They recall some of the historic and profound statements made by Dr. King, and by the actions of Mrs. Rosa Parks. Their presentation of "The Wheels on the Bus" is complimented with African attire.

4. **Nursery and Kindergarten** ... *(singing "The Wheels on the Bus)*

5. Narration by Senior High student #5

   In those days, Black Americans found themselves marching to the tune of "We Shall Overcome" holding hands to form a united front. We remember very well the hymns of the past which celebrated and called to mind the intensity of the struggle for the rights of all people. The Pathfinders Adult class will lead us in singing two well known Spiritual.

6. Songs: Steal Away and O' Freedom.

7. Narration by Senior High student #6:

   In the African-American culture, many artistic ideas and inventions grew out of the need to lighten the work load. Inventions usually came from gifted people who had keen powers of observation and the ability to link together in their minds, the things that would make their work easier. The Primary class will show us some of these.

8. Primary Class presentation ... *(Example are attached)*

9. Narration by Senior High student #7:

   Creation and salvation are two of God's most magnificent wonders. When God made man, He made him in His own image. But through the years, man has questioned, claimed superiority, and denounced inferiority based on race, color and gender. The Primary Junior class brings to us insights in "Black Men in the Bible"

10. Primary Junior class presentation ... *(Some examples are attached)*

11. Narration by Senior High student #8

> Now, we will have Black History Trivia conducted by the Senior High teachers. So put on your thinking caps, and be sure and raise your hands when you think you know the answers.

12. Trivia ... *(See attached)*

13. Narration by Senior High student #9:

> That was fun, and you guys are really sharp. Now when the first African slaves arrived in 1619 on the eastern coast of the United States, they brought with them a rich musical heritage. Their love of music and their need for music in worship and praise to God was the ultimate expression in their daily lives. As they gathered in worship groups, hymns and spirituals, such as "Deep River", "Over My Head, I Hear Music in the Air", "Swing Low, Sweet Chariot", and others were raised to honor God for His goodness and mercy. The Adult classes will close our program in leading us in singing another Spiritual. Thank you all for your participation.

14. Singing ...

15. The Invitation

Teachers should plan their programs not to exceed 5 minutes. Examples are offered as guides, but may be used for actual presentations.

SAMPLE BIOGRAPHIES

Junior High

1

The QUEEN OF SHEBA was a descendant of Cush, a region in Africa inhabited by black people. The Queen ruled an extensive empire consisting of Ethiopia, parts of upper Egypt, and possibly parts of Arabia, Syria, as well as the entire region between the Mediterranean and Erythraean Seas. After hearing of King Solomon's astounding gift of wisdom and prosperity, she traveled the great distance to Jerusalem and there she witnessed the awesome power and majesty of God. She understood that God was the source of King Solomon's greatness. It was this revelation which caused her to submit to the authority of God. She immediately acknowledged God's greatness and went back to her own country praising and blessing His name.

2

SIMON OF CYRENE was a devout Jew from the north African city of Cyrene. He was making his annual pilgrimage to Jerusalem to observe and celebrate the Passover. Many of the Jews from Cyrene were poor. But in spite of their poverty, this Jewish community faithfully sent their tithes to Jerusalem for the upkeep of the Temple. As Simon was passing by on his journey a Roman soldier stopped him and forced him to carry the cross for Jesus. Simon of Cyrene carried the cross to Golgotha, the place where Jesus was crucified and died. Simon was a man who made worship a priority, even though he did not meet Jesus until he carried the cross. And though his journey was interrupted by the Roman soldier, he experienced a greater passion by meeting Jesus face to face. His life was transformed and he returned to his country and shared his knowledge and excitement about Christ with others.

3

SIMEON THE NIGER was a prophet and a teacher at the first Gentile Church at Antioch. His last name is unknown. The word "niger" is the Latin word for Black. Therefore, the Bible calls him Simeon the Black. Black people played an important role in the development of the early church. The church at Antioch proves that God calls leaders from all nations and cultures to spread the Gospel. It was at this church that believers were first called "Christians". Simeon the Niger, along with others, participated in the ordination of Barnabas and Paul commissioning them for the work which God had called them. It is important to listen to God and obey Him. The prophets and ministers at Antioch, including Simeon, listened to God and obeyed. The first missionary journey of Paul got underway, thus spreading the gospel to a large portion of the world at that time.

4

HAGAR was an Egyptian maid and slave who belonged to Abraham and Sarah. They had no children at that time. Even though God told Sarah she would conceive a child, Sarah did not believe God, and gave her slave Hagar to Abraham so that Hagar could produce an heir for the couple. Hagar's pregnancy created intense contempt and animosity between the two women, causing Hagar to flee into the wilderness. In the midst of her flight, the Lord found her and persuaded her to return and to name her son Ishmael. In time, Sarah had her own son as God had promised. But as time passed, Sarah did not want her son Isaac to play with Ishmael, and she insisted that Abraham banish Hagar and her son from the household. Hagar and Ishmael wandered in the wilderness, and when they had no more food or water, she left Ishmael under a bush to die. But God intervened again. He reminded her of His promise to make Ishmael the father of a very large nation. Hagar is a wonderful example of why we should listen and obey God.

5

Jesus looked for ordinary people to become His disciples. He found a leader and a preacher of the Gospel in DR. MARTIN LUTHER KING, JR.; and early in his life, he seemed destined to become a leader in civil rights for his people. Dr. King was one of three children born to Martin Luther King, Sr. and Alberta Williams King. He accepted the pastorate of Dexter Avenue Baptist Church in Montgomery, Alabama. It was here that he made his first mark on the civil rights movement by mobilizing the community for the 382-day boycott of the city's segregated bus system. Dr. King knew that if he could help build a better life for his people, he would have to work with patience and perseverance. Like the apostle Paul in the face of many dangerous missions, Dr. King 'pressed on to the mark of the higher calling'. His solemn plea for peaceful protests and non-violence was just one of the ways he exalted Christ. Many people will forget the violent and turbulent times in the life of Dr. Martin Luther King, Jr., but we will never forget this man of God and his accomplishments.

SOME TOOLS MADE AND USED BY SLAVES

Primary Class

The ironing board

Mops

Brooms

Sculptured bowls and cups

Hand axes

Hammers and mallets

and many others

SAMPLE: SOME BLACK MEN IN THE BIBLE

Primary Junior Class

First Speaker:	What are you guys doing here?
Second:	We're comparing notes.
Third:	Our Sunday School teacher asked us to find evidence of the Black Man in the Bible.
Fourth:	Yes, and I found that the original man, Adam, was formed from the dust of the earth in Eden, which is in Africa. That makes Adam the forefather of all men.
Fifth:	And I found in Genesis that only eight people boarded the Ark that Noah built. Noah was a black man. The flood destroyed all life except his family, and the earth was replenished with people from his family line. Wouldn't that make all people related by blood?
Sixth:	Did you know that the ancient Pharoahs and rulers were great African Kings, and considered to be gods among their people?
Seventh:	Listen to this: Moses was a black man, and he led the Hebrew people under God's direction out of Egypt where they were made slaves to Pharoah. God used Moses to perform many miracles so that Pharoah and his people would know that God was the only true God.
Eighth:	Well, I think that one of the greatest miracles was the gigantic temple Solomon built for God in Jerusalem. First Kings tells us he did it without the sound of the hammer, axe, or tools

of iron in the construction. And you know the Black Canaanite harlot Rahab was his ancestor.

Ninth: And what about Jesus who performed the greatest miracle of all. He lived without sin, and paid the price for our sin on the cross. He died and rose again. No one can top that!

First Speaker: I think our teacher will be pleased with this assignment. Let's go.

BIBLE AND BLACK HISTORY TRIVIA

1. Who was the world's longest living man? _Methuselah – 969 years_

2. Who was the woman created from Adam's rib? _Eve._

3. Who was the woman responsible for the underground railroad? _Harriet Tubman_

4. Jesus raised this man from the dead. _Lazarus_

5. Who was the man who persecuted Christians before he was converted? _Saul / Paul_

6. Who was the first African American Supreme Court Justice? _Thurgood Marshall_

7. Who was the non-violent activist working for human and civil rights in the 1960s? _Dr. Martin Luther King, Jr._

8. Who was the first black female tennis player to win Wimbledon? _Althea Gibson_

9. Who was the black man who helped Jesus carry the cross to Golgotha? _Simon of Cyrene_

10. The famous championship boxer who was born Casius Clay and changed his name to … _Mohammad Ali_

11. What is the name of the last Book of the Bible? _Revelations_

12. Who is the President of South Africa who spent much of his life in prison? _Nelson Mandela_

13. How many disciples did Jesus call first to follow Him? _Twelve_

14. Can you name the disciples? _Peter, Andrew, James, John, Philip, Bartholomew,Thomas, Matthew, James, son of Alphaeus, Thaddaeus, Simon the Zealot, Judas Iscariot_

15. What are the four Gospel Books of the Bible? *Matthew, Mark, Luke, John*

16. Who is the famous surgeon, born in Detroit, Michigan, who pioneered brain surgery on many children? *Dr. Ben Carson, M.D.*

Portraits in Black

Biographies of men and women who are playing, or have played a role in the shaping of America

BLACK HISTORY PROGRAM
Plans for the Performers

1. Select a person who has made a significant contribution to Black History to study and portray.

2. Write a brief biography to read or recite (approximately one page handwritten or one-half page typewritten.

   a. You are that person
   b. Your speech will be "I am ...
   c. You will dress as that person dressed

Example:

> My name is Mary McCleod Bethune. I was born in Mayesville, South Carolina where I attended a mission school, a seminary, and was further educated at Moody Bible School. I am the first black woman to head a federal office, and to be appointed to various government posts under 4 presidents ... etc.

You might wish to portray a famous person who is still alive; i.e., Nelson Mandela, Rosa Parks, etc. You will need to do some research so that your speech and mannerism will closely depict that person.

- As soon as you have selected your person to portray, contact the director for assistance in costuming.

- Your speech should be edited for authenticity, and suggestions for a good performance.

(Sample Biographies are attached)

SET

Left Stage:	A podium with a microphone
Portable Props:	A chair and stand for Madame Walker; straightening comb and curling irons.
Right Stage:	**A picture frame constructed and decorated, large enough to frame each character for a photo shoot before leaving the stage.**
Photographer:	Stationed where a photo can be made of each character in the picture frame before exiting.

(Diagram)

Each member of the cast dressed to portray the Character enters at Stage Left. The speeches are delivered from the podium at Stage Left. The exit is at Stage Right after the photo shoot in the picture frame.

Cues for entry are prompted by the narration.

Portraits In Black
Characters

Martin Luther King, Jr. ____________

Rosa Parks ____________

Harriet Tubman ____________

Nelson Mandela ____________

Negro Folk Singer ____________

Madame C. J. Walker ____________

Thurgood Marshall ____________

Coleman A. Young ____________

Dr. Ben Carson, M.D. ____________

Mahalia Jackson ____________

James Earl Jones ____________

Althea Gibson ____________

Oprah Winfrey ____________

Maya Angelou ____________

Judith Jamison ____________

James Cleveland ____________

Portraits in Black
Narrative

Narrator:
Good evening! Welcome to Portraits in Black, presented by the Charles G. Adams Drama Group. Our program features a look back into the history of Africa and America, the struggle for freedom, triumphs and achievements. We will explore a rich legacy of pride from the realms of slavery and civil rights, to justice and freedom. Also, the American way of life, from the rise of the anti-slavery movements to a more current status and progress. We begin with the celebrated force in the civil rights movement from 1957 to 1968. There were many travels, many demonstrations, many speeches, all of which are noteworthy. But the final speech at Ebenezer Baptist Church in Atlanta, Georgia, on February 4, l968, has a message which should challenge us forever.

Martin Luther King, Jr. enters and speaks ...

Narrator:
The Civil Rights Movement of the '60s opened doors for the Civil Rights Act of 1964. The major catalyst in this movement was marked by a courageous black woman who dared to defy the segregated transportation system of Montgomery, Alabama.

Rosa Parks enters and speaks ...

Narrator:
There is no question that African-Americans have struggled to obtain the very basic rights. It is a struggle that spanned the centuries – from the mutinies by African slaves during the Atlantic crossing, to insurrections organized by slaves in the New World. We remember Nat Turner, leader of the insurrections; Frederick Douglas, abolitionist; Sojourner Truth and the struggle for women's rights. And then there was Harriet Tubman and her outstanding display of courage.

Harriet Tubman enters and speaks ...

Narrator:
Twenty years, and then freedom. Freedom for a man who had been brought up to respect and hold on to family values, and only to watch the tradition slip away blatantly in apartheid. Families were forced to live apart in their struggle for survival. Nelson Mandela walked out of the prison gates and onto the world stage.

Nelson Mandela enters and speaks ...

Narrator:
Africans arriving on the eastern shores brought with them a rich musical heritage. Many of their songs reflect the life of a slave, hand times, and praises to God who would keep them in spite of hardships.

Negro Folk Singer enters and sings "O Freedom"

Narrator:
It was Book T. Washington who first saw the possibility of securing African-American economic stability through business development. So he spearheaded the National Negro Business League to encourage Black entrepreneurs. The belief was, when an individual produces what the world wants, the world does not stop to inquire about the skin color of the producer. This woman of color had 'true grit', and a plan.

Madame C. J. Walker enters, seats her customer
and speaks ...

Narrator:
The Civil Rights Movement brought together blacks and sympathetic whites as nothing had ever done before, but not without a price. School desegregation, voting rights, and the right to work laws brought about strife. In many cases, civil rights legislation was being challenged all the way to the Supreme Court. More and more African-American Attorneys and Justices were making their debut. In 1967, the first African-American was appointed to the highest court in the land, the United States Supreme Court.

Thurgood Marshall enters and speaks ...

Narrator:
Over several decades, African-Americans have been elected and selected for political offices in increasing numbers. Significant among them was the first black woman, Carole Mosely Braun, to the United States Senate. In 1992, there were 39 African-Americans occupying seats in Congress. President Clinton added 7 to his cabinet. African-American Mayors were elected in large cities: Maynard Jackson, Andrew Young, David Dinkins, Thomas Bradley, Harold Washington, and our own Mayor of Detroit, Coleman Alexander Young.

Coleman A. Young enters and speaks ...

Narrator:
For many years, the progress of African-Americans in Science and Medicine was deliberately hidden. But medical schools such as Howard University, Meharry Medical College, and Atlanta University continued to train and research. Then we began to hear of Charles Drew and blood plasma research, Ulysses Grant Daily and Daniel Hale Williams for open heart surgery. Here in Detroit, we claim a native son who has recorded major strides in surgery.

Dr. Ben Carson enters and speaks ...

Narrator:
As the years passed, song writers kept the tradition alive with folk songs and spirituals such as, O, Freedom, Steal Away, Over My Head, I see Trouble in the Air. Mahalia Jackson will always be remembered as the world's greatest gospel singer. She toured Europe and sang at London's Albert Hall where she won awards. Many of you will remember that she sang at the 1963 March on Washington, as well as at the funeral of Dr. Martin Luther King, Jr.

Mahalia Jackson enters and sings 'O When the Saints Go Marching In'.

Narrator:
As the Civil Rights Movement challenged the National conscience in the '60s, every facet of Afro-American life began to change, including Performing Arts. More plays about African-Americans were produced by both Black and White playwrights. Dramatic actors of color began appearing on Broadway, including the man with the resonant voice, James Earl Jones.

James Earl Jones enters and speaks ...

Narrator:
Of all the sports, basketball seemed to offer the greatest future for African-Americans. Now diversity extends to most areas of professional and amateur sports. African-Americans have excelled at the Olympic Games. But at the management level of sports, the progress is still slow. The untimely death of Arthur Ashe in 1993 robbed the black community of a pioneering sports hero who was an avid spokesman for young athletes. Women also have claimed prominent places in sports.

Althea Gibson enters and speaks ...

Narrator:
In the early '30s, Journalism in the form of newspaper and magazine publishing was progressive. Representation in the broadcasting industry increased as the years passed. In 1962, Mal Goode became the first African-American network TV reporter at ABC-TV. Since that time, Tony Brown, Ed Bradley, Bryant Gumbel, Carole Simpson, and others have moved ahead as television journalists. The next lady has distinguished herself to produce the ultimate in Talk Shows.

Oprah Winfrey enters and speaks ...

Narrator:
Marguerite Johnson spent her formative years shuffling between St. Louis, Missouri, San Francisco, and a tiny little segregated town in Arkansas. She became Maya Angelou when she realized how firm

she had set her goals. Life was rough growing up. You only have to read the first volume of her autobiography, "I Know Why The Caged Bird Sings": to see the problems she faced. Maya's poetry seems to be as much a part of her autobiography as the succeeding volumes. As one writer says, 'it is not fiction, it is true life'. Many of us will remember on January 20, 1993, Maya recited her poem entitled, "On The Pulse Of The Morning" during the inauguration of President Clinton. Now we will hear "And Still, I Rise".

Maya Angelou enters and recites 'And Still, I Rise".

Narrator:
In 1958, Alvin Ailey formed his own dance group, The Alvin Ailey American Dance Theater, and won international fame. Judith Jamison, who had studied dance since she was six years old, was discovered by Agnes DeMille. Judith joined the Ailey Group as a principal dancer. She won high honors on Broadway in the hit, Sophisticated Ladies, which featured the music of Duke Ellington.

Judith Jamison dances...

Narrator:
The Reverend James Cleveland, known by such titles as 'King James' and the 'Crown Prince' emerged as a giant on the postwar gospel music scene. Just as Mahalia Jackson and many others, James Cleveland first sang gospel under the direction of Thomas Dorsey, at Pilgrim Baptist Church in Chicago. At the height of his career, he organized annual conventions that brought thousands of gospel singers, choirs and song writers together in great celebrations.

Rev. James Cleveland sings "The Love of God".

Narrator:
We do hope you have enjoyed this presentation. Thank you for

being a great audience. And now we invite you to join us for a reception in the Fellowship Hall. We know you will want to meet these wonderful players. Let's give them another round of applause.

The End

DR. MARTIN LUTHER KING, JR.
Excerpts from the sermon preached at
Ebenezer Baptist Church in Atlanta
February 4, 1968

This evening let us talk about the Drum Major instinct. We all know what part the drum major plays in the band. It is a place of importance. We all want to be important, to surpass others, to achieve distinction, and to lead the parade. But there comes a time when the drum major instinct can become destructive. It can cause one's personality to become distorted. Some people have a need to feel superior ... some have a need to feel that they are first. These are the needs that can cause racial struggle, and has caused struggle between nations.

But Jesus gave us a new norm for greatness when He said, "He who is greatest among you shall be your servant". You only need a heart full of grace, and a soul generated by love.

And every now and then I think about my own death. When that time comes, I'd like somebody to mention that Martin Luther King, Jr. tried to give his life serving others. If you say I was a drum major, say that I was a drum major for justice, say that I was a drum major for peace; I was a drum major for righteousness. And all the other shallow things will not matter. I won't have any money to leave behind. I won't have the fine things of life to leave behind. But I just want to leave the memory of a committed life behind.

ROSA PARKS
Civil Rights Activist

My name is Rosa Parks. I guess you could say I am the Civil Rights Activist who started the transportation revolution in Montgomery, Alabama. You see, I was tired of my rights and the rights and dignity of black people being pushed around and demeaned. So when that bus driver ordered me to move to the back of the bus so that a white man could sit down, I just sat there. My actions set off the longest transportation boycott in history. It lasted 382 days.

I was raised in Tuskegee and Montgomery, Alabama by my mother and grandparents who taught me to be a strong and respectable young lady. I passed through segregated schools with honors, and attended the all black Alabama State College. I was taught to be proud of my heritage.

I met the young minister, Martin Luther King, Jr. during the struggle and the marches. His determination and work for the rights of African Americans will always be remembered. Those who marched and died with him will take their places in history as National Heroes. But I don't feel like a hero.

I moved to Detroit in 1957 because of the threats and continued problems in the aftermath. But I am still working for the cause of justice, and I promise to do so as long as I live.

MADAME C. J. WALKER

Entrepreneur

I was born Sarah Breedlove in Delta, Louisiana. But the world knows me as Madame C. J. Walker. You should never forget me, for I am America's first self-made millionaire.

I was orphaned as a child and raised by my sister in Vicksburg, Mississippi. In my early teens, I got tired of working in kitchens and laundries, and watching black women struggle with their appearance, especially their hair. So I began working to develop the hot comb. At 37 years of age, and with $1.50 in my pocket, I moved to Denver, Colorado and started a hair preparation company. I married C. J. Walker, a journalist, who taught me advertising and mail order promotion.

I developed a hair care system that gave dry hair a soft texture. Millions of women, both black and white, became customers. In 1910, I moved to Indianapolis, Indiana and established a factory and a laboratory, and hired hundreds of workers. I developed a nation-wide network of 5,000 sales agents, mostly Africa-American women, and had more than 2,000 agents marketing my ever expanding line of products. Many are still being used today.

The legacy I leave to young people is this: It doesn't take a rich man to start a business. It takes education, determination, and communication. Get a good plan and go for it!

THURGOOD MARSHALL

U.S. Supreme Court Justice

I am Thurgood Marshall, the first African American to be appointed to the highest Court in the land – the U. S. Supreme Court. I was 59 years of age at the time, and had already built a history of leadership in law, especially in the NAACP organization.

I was born in Baltimore, Maryland – the son of a sleeping car porter, and the grandson of a slave. I started a career in dentistry after graduating from Lincoln University, but changed my mind and entered Howard University Law School. Immediately, I began working with the NAACP.

As Attorney Marshall, I started a private practice and became National Special Counsel to handle all cases involving constitutional rights of African Americans. As a member of the National Bar Association, I had a license to participate in important cases and counsels all over the country. I received more than 20 honorary degrees from universities in this country as well as in other countries.

But my work with the U. S. Supreme Court is most noteworthy. Of the thirty-two cases I argued, I won twenty-nine. I believe the fight for the rights of African Americans must continue until the dream of Dr. Martin Luther King, Jr. has been totally realized. Then, and only then will history be correctly recorded.

COLEMAN ALEXANDER YOUNG
Former Mayor of Detroit, Michigan

Good evening. I am Coleman A. Young, the first African-American mayor of Detroit. My term of office was one of the longest running terms, from 1973 to 1993, and I left a rich record of progress.

I was born into a family of educators. My mother was a teacher, so I did not have a choice of going, or not going to school. We moved from southern Alabama to Detroit, into the neighborhood known as Black Bottom.

You bet the city progressed under Coleman Young's twenty years in office. I believe in progress, and believe me, I got the city moving, even though sometimes I had to use some, shall we say, <u>rough</u> language! But I was able to get surrounding communities to work with me in many areas. Oh yes, I complained that bigotry was my worst enemy. But I also bragged that I was the only Mayor of a big city ever arrested for protesting against apartheid in South Africa. People say I bring race into any topic, But I don't believe in hatred, and I think that should be known.

I retired from office in 1993, but still support the progress of the city of Detroit.

JAMES EARL JONES
Actor

I am James Earl Jones, the actor. I was born in Tate County, Mississippi, but was raised by my grandparents on a farm near Jackson, Michigan. As far as being educated is concerned, 'to be or not to be' was never an option, according to my grandmother. I graduated cum laude in 1953 as a pre-medical student from the University of Michigan.

Acting was in my blood. You see, my father was an actor. I moved to New York after graduation and studied at the American

Theater Wing. I learned early that nothing comes easy, especially for a black man. So I had to be better than good!

I first appeared on Broadway in "The Great White Hope". Oh, what an experience! After that, I began appearing in roles traditionally performed by white actors, such as the title role in "King Lear", and the award winning performance in Steinbeck's "Of Mice And Men", and many others. The most memorable television appearance was portraying Alex Haley in "Roots: The Next Generation".

If James Earl Jones' legacy is to be left for young black children, it is this: 'Prepare yourselves with a good education; then be the best you can be in whatever you plan for your life'.

BEN CARSON, M.D.

Surgeon

Dr. Ben Carson should be a familiar name to many people in Detroit, for I am a native Detroiter. I attended Detroit Public Schools, and suffered through as many, and maybe more problems than you could ever imagine. You see, my family was very poor. My brother and I were raised by a mom who did the best she could. She only had a third grade education, and good jobs that paid real money to raise a family just were not there for her.

I attended Southwestern High School and soon became very much aware that our standard of living was far below that of my peers. Consequently, my clothing caused laughter and ridicule. It was then that I started defending my honor with my fists. But I realized I had to change my behavior after I almost killed my best friend in a fist fight. I was so remorseful that I found a Bible and started reading it every day.

My mother told me of a vision she had that one day I would be a doctor. And from that day, I started working toward that goal. My whole outlook on life and my attitude towards clothes and things changed.

Now you might call me a legend because I have performed many seemingly impossible surgeries. And with the help of God, I pioneered brain surgery on more than thirty children who had no other hope of survival.

One of my greatest loves is spending time talking with children and teaching them how to set goals; how to avoid drugs and dangerous habits; how to rise above bad family situations; and how to use their God-given talents and abilities to be the very best they can be.

ALTHEA GIBSON

Tennis Player

Hello! My name is Althea Gibson, the tennis Pro. It seems that tennis has always been a part of my life. As a girl in Silver, South Carolina, I learned to play paddle tennis. When we moved to Harlem, New York, I began entering tennis tournaments and won the Manhattan Department of Parks Girls Championship. I was so excited! At 15 years of age, I began receiving professional coaching. In 1945 and 1946, I won the National Negro Girls Singles Championship.

At Florida A & M University, I received scholarships for tennis and basketball. In 1950, I was the first Black to play tennis at Forest Hill, and in 1951, I played at Wimbledon. In 1957, I won the Wimbledon Singles Crown, and with Darlene Hart, won the doubles championship. Also in 1957 and 1958, I won the U.S. Open Women's Singles. That was another highlight of my life!

As far back as I can remember, I always wanted to be somebody. If you would read my book entitled "I Always Wanted To Be Somebody" you will learn more about how I became somebody in the world of sports. You can do it, too. Just go out and do it!

HARRIET TUBMAN
Slave

I know most of you have heard about me in your lifetime. My name is Harriet Tubman. I was born a slave in 1821 on a plantation in Dorchester County, Maryland. I became rebellious against the slave system early in life because of the abuse I suffered and inhumane treatment I saw happening to other slaves.

At 28 years of age, I escaped and fled to the North. Immediately, I developed a plan to free 300 slaves, including my parents. So intense was my determination in freeing the slaves, people began calling me 'Moses'. Now ain't that something! Because of my knowledge of the country, I became the conductor of the Underground Railroad. The next ten years, I made twenty trips to the South and rescued many more slaves. My reputation grew, and eventually a $40,000 reward was posted for my capture.

In 1860, I began to canvas the nation, appearing at anti-slavery meetings and speaking on women's rights. Shortly before the Civil War, I was forced to leave Canada and return to the United States. I have no regrets to this day for my actions.

NELSON MANDELA
President of South Africa

I am Nelson Mandela, today a free man. Free from the South African jail where I was incarcerated for the struggle for freedom. And now, many of my dreams have come true for the South African black people. I am the son of a tribal chief, and just as my father, I have dedicated my life to fighting for the freedom of my people.

As a boy, I studied tribal history. I learned that many times my ancestors were forced to fight against each other, but still I held onto the importance of kinship. I knew that before white men came to South Africa, all men were free. And so I set out to reclaim that heritage.

At 43 years of age, I was arrested for encouraging black workers to go on strike and leave the country without a passport. I, and three other men were captured and taken to prison, to an island formerly used to isolate a colony of lepers and other people with incurable diseases. But even in jail, I would not be talked down to, and this caused the wardens much stress. I soon learned that what should have been a five year sentence stretched into nearly three decades in a jail cell. I was the world's most famous prisoner.

I believe, and I will work for the time when slavery, poverty, want, and servitude shall be no more. I am dedicated to this cause. This struggle is my life.

OPRAH WINFREY

Talk Show Host/Actress/Broadcasting Executive

Hello, out there! My name is Oprah Winfrey – as if you didn't know! Let me tell you a little bit about myself!

I was born in a little town called Kosciusco, Mississippi. When I was a little girl, my life was a mess and I don't want to talk about that. But I got on track when at fourteen years old, I went to live with my father in Nashville, Tennessee. I attended school every day because he was a "mean" man. I earned a B.A. Degree from Tennessee State University and became a reporter at WTVF-TV. From 1976 to 1983, I lived in Baltimore where I became news anchor on WJZ-TV, and soon moved on to co-host a popular show called "People Are Talking". In 1984, I moved to Chicago, where I kept a dying show called "A.M. Chicago" alive. And then, guess what? It was so successful that we changed the name to "The Oprah Winfrey Show". You know, I've been told it is now the most popular television talk show in history. Now ain't that something!
And don't forget, I am a talented, mind you, a talented actress! Remember "The Color Purple"? And the television movie "The Women of Brewster Place"? That's me, child!

I can't say this often enough; if you want something bad enough, go out and get it. Do it the right way, of course. There's no limit to what you can achieve if you are determined and you're willing to work hard for it!

WHAT ABOUT MY ATTITUDE?

Questions asked by young people
who have just accepted Christ.

Many times when young people accept Christ, we take for granted that they are well aware of what Salvation is all about. Often times children are misled into thinking that this is the place they can come and have fun. Some want to join their friends who sing in the choir; some would like to become members of the Drama Group; and some might feel they have no other place to go on certain nights and on Sunday mornings. As Christian youth leaders, we believe it is the role of the church to provide Christian nurture and an atmosphere of Christian growth through prayer, Bible study, training in worship, and other wholesome activities.

This conversation between a Sunday School teacher and a student was written and videotaped for use in group sessions.

Many times Christians have questions concerning the decision they have just made about Salvation. This is especially true of young people. Some of their concerns are:

1. How do I know Christ really came into my heart when I asked Him to?

2. Am I supposed to look and act differently so God can approve of me?

3. How am I supposed to feel?

4. What should I do if friends question or reject me?

5. How often should I discuss my new life with parents and others?

6. How does God view my attitude and behavior?

Becoming a Christian is the beginning of a wonderful new life. A whole new world is unfolding. It's kind of like a bird hatching from an egg. And just being hatched is not enough. You need to grow and eventually learn how to fly. These questions will be answered as you mature in Christ. Your Sunday School teachers are waiting to help you. Reading your Bible, and your communication with God are the sources of power to grow. Let's listen to a conversation between a young Christian and his teacher.

****

TEACHER: Hello, James!

JAMES: Hi!

TEACHER: I understand you joined the church a few weeks ago and you have some questions.

JAMES: Yes. I'm afraid so.

TEACHER: Okay, let's talk. You ask, and I will try to answer. If I don't have the answer, I will consult someone else, and together we will consult God's word.

JAMES: Okay. I know I asked Christ to come into my heart, but how can I be sure He did, and He is now in my life?

TEACHER: Let's go back over a few things. When you asked Jesus to come into your heart, you also confessed that you are a sinner. And remember, this is so, based on Romans 3:23. "For all have sinned and come short of the glory of God"

JAMES: Yes, I know.

TEACHER: And you believe that Jesus Christ died on the cross for our sins?

JAMES: I believe.

TEACHER: And that He was buried, but rose on the third day. He is now seated with the Father in heaven taking care of our prayers and concerns.

JAMES: That's awesome!

TEACHER: Then Romans 10:9 confirms our salvation. *(Read from the Bible)*

JAMES: Okay. But suppose I call on Him sometimes and can't seem to find Him; especially when I need Him to help me with a real problem?

TEACHER: If you feel you can't find God when you need Him most, remember this: It is <u>your</u> will that God is interested in. If you are sincere about wanting Christ to take over your life, say so to Him. Read your Bible and believe that He will do just that. In Hebrews 13:5 God says, "Never will I leave you; never will I forsake you".

JAMES: I felt good when I accepted Christ. It was like all my problems were suddenly gone. But sometimes now I feel alone, like I've lost God.

TEACHER: You must remember, God answers prayers in His own time and His own way. He might not give you what you want, but He will always provide what you need. Solving your problems His way is always the best.

JAMES: I guess I can understand that.

TEACHER: We are only human, and we are going to waiver in our feelings and thinking sometimes. But God is divine, and He never goes back on His word. Hebrews 13:8 says, "Jesus Christ is the same yesterday and today and forever".

JAMES: That's good news!

TEACHER: You know, God has others out there working for Him. When you find a good Christian friend, discuss these feelings with that friend. We don't always know who God is using to help us.

JAMES: I've been trying to be a good Christian since I made this decision, but sometimes I'm still not sure He accepts me even after I pray.

TEACHER: A lot of people often feel this way. This is going to depend on your communication with God. Let's examine how you talk to God. Do you feel He is right there listening? Remember, you have already asked Him to come into your heart and be your Savior.

Open your Bible to Romans 8:26,27. *(Read)* Your complete trust in God when you pray will call up the Spirit of God.

JAMES: It seems I have a lot of work to do to really become a Christian.

TEACHER: Remember, you don't have to work at becoming a Christian because Christ has already accepted <u>you</u>. All you have to do is work at growing by reading you Bible, communicating with God, and talking with other Christians about your experiences. Don't forget to share with your parents.

JAMES: Oh, no! How can I forget my parents? You see, it's not easy talking with them. Too often when we try to discuss something, we end up on a battle ground. They don't listen to me.

TEACHER: I'll bet you feel like you are the victim and your parents are the enemy.

JAMES: You got it! They just don't seem to understand and agree with me.

TEACHER: You know, James, Jesus said to love your enemies, and honor your father and mother. And when we try very hard to do what He asks us to do, then He will make it easier. Don't forget, God also works through parents.

JAMES: Why does Jesus give us the hard jobs?

TEACHER: Well, He understands us and many times He calls upon us to do specific things just to prove that we are ready to love <u>Him</u>. Take a look at Proverbs 15:1 *(Read)* Does that sound like He is trying to teach us?

JAMES: That's neat! But how did you find all these answers?

TEACHER: It takes time and help from your Sunday School teachers, your pastor, and many others as you move from a hatched egg and begin to develop your wings.

JAMES: My world doesn't seem to have changed. I mean, I still go to school and I study. I am a good student. The only thing that seems to have changed is how my friends treat me.

TEACHER: Are you bothered by the way your friends relate to you now?

JAMES: It's like they are afraid of me, or they feel they can't talk to me freely like old times.

TEACHER: Have you examined the 'old times' relationships? Do you now want to talk about the things you used to talk about with them?

JAMES: Well, we did do a lot of talking about people. I suppose God would call that gossiping. I'm sure I don't want to do that anymore. Does God know that about me?

TEACHER: He certainly does. You see, God knows everything about you, even though you have not told Him some things in your confession. Remember, He knew you even before you confessed. But He still forgives you when you ask Him to.

JAMES: I know. I have another concern. Sometimes kids like to pick on me. Everybody knows I will ... well, stand up for myself. I've been in a few fights.

TEACHER: Do you remember why Jesus went to the cross? He has taken care of the past experiences you have had, good and bad.

JAMES: Oh, great! I know I don't want to go there again.

TEACHER: Matthew 5:39 tells us to turn the other cheek. That might be a hard one, especially when you are being picked on. But you need to plan some specific actions to get around this. I once heard a young man say to a bully while holding up both hands; "Hey, I'm not a fighter. I think you have the wrong guy". The bully walked away.

JAMES: That might work sometimes because some kids are just bullies.

TEACHER: That's why you need to work on some responses you think Jesus might make. It takes time, but some good information can be found in the Gospel of John, chapters 14-17; the Book of James, and the Book of Proverbs. Don't be surprised if a little change in your attitude and behavior causes a big change in people you consider the enemy.

JAMES: My best friend seems to be moving away from God even though he says he has accepted Him. He wants me to follow him, only I don't think I want to do the same things I did before I accepted Christ. We used to play around after school ... Well, how can I stop him?

TEACHER: Maybe you can't. In the world today, there are so many terrible persuasions. The songs with bad messages, unsavory programs on TV, peer pressure, especially from the opposite sex.

JAMES: Most of the friends I used to hang with are on my case.

TEACHER: It would be nice if you could teach them all you know. But try praying for them first. Just continue to live as much like Christ as you can. This way you are showing them the Fruits of the Spirit as found in Galatians 5:22-23. Let's read it. *(Read)*

JAMES: Oh, my!

TEACHER: But don't fool yourself. God just might want you to make choices about who you hang around with.

JAMES: Yes. That might not be a bad idea. That sounds simple.

TEACHER: It really is not simple, and we have to work at it. We have a guide. It's sort of like when you and your family are traveling to a place you have never been before. You have a road map, but if you don't study it, you will get lost. The Bible is our guide. Study it and follow Jesus' examples and you will grow as a Christian.

JAMES: I understand.

TEACHER: Remember, our hope for growth as Christians is based on our understanding who we are as children of God. How you understand your identity makes a big difference in your success in dealing with the challenges and conflicts in your life. Know your relationship with God.

JAMES: It sounds like my daily walk with Christ could be like my relationship with a good and true friend.

TEACHER: I couldn't have said it better myself. Your Christian walk is the direct result of what you believe about God and yourself. If your faith is off, then your walk will be out of step. And don't be afraid to tackle problems like rejection and criticism. Remember, we could never suffer like Jesus suffered for us. There will always be issues you don't agree with. But keep the faith. Why not keep this prayer with you and read it often.

JAMES: *(Reads)* "God grant me the serenity to accept the things I cannot change ... The courage to change the things I can ... And the wisdom to know the difference."

Gosh! Thank you so much

TEACHER: Anytime.

Miscellaneous

Selections

The
Retreat

As much as we were enjoying the first fellowship after our arrival, this period finally drifted away with the deacon's resonant voice saying, "Let us pray". The prayer of thanksgiving for the assembly and a safe trip was stimulating. We knew we had to get up early the next morning even though we were late arriving at the retreat site, but no one seemed ready to go to bed. So we stood around visiting and exchanging joyous anticipation of the weekend ahead of us. Gradually the crowd began to diminish as retreat members said their 'goodnights' and soon we all headed for our assigned private rooms.

As I entered my room, I was pleasantly surprised at how quaint and comfortable it was. I walked over to the window. There was nothing to see outside except the lighted parking area. Beyond that, it was dark. I could tell we were not in the heart of a city, or even close to one. After all, this was rural America where man's ingenuity and ambition had not manned the jackhammers, cement mixers, and scaffolds to intrude upon the serenity of this place. Where is this place? I do not know. I only know we had driven approximately four hours up to Northern Michigan. And the farther we drove, the less populated we found the area.

I felt sleepy, so I unpacked my bags, stepped into a quick shower and donned my nightgown. Strangely enough, habits do not take a holiday when you leave home. I said my prayers, then I felt compelled to read the Bible in spite of my need for sleep. So I propped up in bed and open my Bible to Psalm 8.

> *"O Lord, our Lord, how excellent is thy name in all the earth! Who hast set thy glory above the heavens ..."*

This is my Psalm of praise. Each time I read it, I experience a peace that passes all understanding. I closed the Book and sleep came quickly.

At the break of dawn, I opened my eyes and saw faint outlines of objects in my room. Funny how I had not paid close attention to the room last night. The window, of course, allowed the dim light to seep through. There was a table in the corner with a small mirror over it, a closet without a door that housed my weekend gear, a comfortable stuffed chair, and beside it, a night stand with a pole lamp protruding out of its center.

I got up and walked to the window in time to see the gradual emergence of light make sense of the shadows in the distance. To the right, there was a line of trees. Some were skinny; after all, this was October and the few leaves that were left were brown and ready to fall as soon as the breeze came through. The scarlet and gold of fall had faded. The evergreens were the darkest shadows until the light finally revealed their identity. In front of me, there was a wide expanse of play area with a catcher screen. I pressed my face to the window to see as far as I could to the left. There was a rather rugged incline leveling off to what looked like park benches; two, or maybe there were three of them spaced several feet apart. And the trees were ample to provide shade in spring and summer. I wasn't aware I had been standing there so long until I realized that the sun must be rising on the eastern horizon behind the building. The light jolted me into the reality of the day. I rushed to shower and dress, remembering the 7:00 a.m. breakfast. Then our day really begins.

Breakfast was good, complete with bacon, eggs, toast, jelly, hash browns, cereal and fruit, and coffee. What a way to begin the day. The cheery buzzing of morning greetings and exchanges were refreshing. Our numbers seemed to have multiplied. And then I remembered we had been joined by one-day retreat members. The minister who would co-direct the retreat was brilliant in setting the stage for our activities. Prayer was reverent and quieting. Blessings were so evident as she quietly talked to God, asking Him to bless the food and renew our whole being.

The morning session was complete with singing, praying, Bible study, and preaching. The spirit was high as testimonies were more personal than I had witnessed before in our congregation.

After lunch, we were given an hour to return to the quiet of our rooms and read scriptures of our choice. And then we were to explore the grounds and commune individually with God and nature. At 3:00 p.m., we were directed to return to the assembly room for a period of sharing. Before I reached my room, I knew I would read Psalm 139. It cried out to me and filled my whole body with comfort and joy. Oh, how I love to reflect upon God, and how fearfully and wonderfully I am made.

> *"O Lord, you have searched me and you know me. You know when I sit and when I rise, you perceive my thoughts from afar. You discern my going out and my lying down; you are familiar with all my ways ..."*

And the prayer goes on and on. I read it again and then I talked with God. I felt good, like I was talking with a friend. After all, He knew all about me and could perceive what was in my mind. As I put on my walking shoes, I thought, 'how good it is to be alone with God'.

The air was fresh, not cold, but cool enough for the sweater I brought. What a sight! It seemed we had traveled to a place where man had built a little residence just large enough to hold a few hundred people. And there really was nothing close by except trees and earth and sky. I was so busy taking it all in, I hardly noticed the people spread out all over the area, walking, sitting on the grass, or standing alone.

As I moved slowly through the parked cars and out to one of the many paths that networked the grounds, I was thinking, 'O God, how great you are. You have made this great big world, and all that is in it, and just for us. How great and caring you are'. I walked slowly and deliberately toward the trees, inhaling with vigor the fresh air as though I could consume enough to last a lifetime. As I reached the edge where the trees were rather dense, I could hear a rustling among the leaves. For sure that was a little animal there; probably hiding itself to be safe. I waited for him to come out, but I could hear him moving away from me. I walked on. Some birds flew about in the trees. It was as though they had come to welcome me and to tell me the secrets of serenity at this place. I imagined they were saying:

"Look! Here we are up here. This land and air are free. Run and play and enjoy yourself. The freedom of life is delicious. Enjoy! Enjoy! Cheep, cheep!"

I smiled at their cheerfulness and walked on.

And then a squirrel appeared. He was scampering here and there among the leaves in a playful manner. And then there were more. I thought the little scamp I heard before went out and summoned his friends to come and see me. There were three brown ones and one was grey. If they weren't a family, it made no difference. They chased each other up and down the trees. I asked aloud, "Why are you so happy"? They stopped at the sound of my voice as if to answer:

"We don't have a care in the world. Our food is provided as the nuts fall from the trees. God watches over us and provides for us just as He does for you. Why wouldn't we enjoy this freedom?" And they scampered away.

Wow! I walked on slowly admiring God's creation. As I moved on to a larger group of trees, I was anxiously anticipating the next message I would receive. I slowed my pace for a closer observation. Some of the trees were huge birch, oak, and maple. Many had lost all their beautiful brown and gold leaves, but still stood tall and handsome reaching toward the sky. Interspersed within and closer to the edges were evergreens of various shapes and sizes. Some were sharply topped and shaped perfectly like Christmas trees. Others were sprawling as if to protect their spaces. I looked up to clear my vision of the density below, and to my surprise, a breeze was passing quietly through and gently stirring their peace. As I stood there, I wondered how God had caused them to sprout and grow up together. It was then that I imagined the oak talking quietly to the birch:

"Are you enjoying this peace?"

The birch replied, "Yes, but I am fast falling asleep".

There was a chuckle from a sharply topped evergreen.

"What is this?" I asked. "What is so amusing?"

The evergreen ignored me and said to the others, "You guys are all wiped out for the season, and now you fall asleep."

The maple stirred. "Listen to you, young thing! God is good to us. He allows us to rest during the cold. Many times He covers us with a blanket of snow, and He keeps us during the storms and the rain. So there".

The evergreen replied, "Yes, but you sleep as though you are dead creatures. Now we are bright and wide awake to enjoy all seasons. Can you top that goodness of God?"

The oak replied, "Peace, my brother. This sleep is perfect peace."

The maple added, "And how good it is in spring when God sees fit to wake us. Can't you just hear the 'oohs' and 'aahs' as people pass by and exclaim at the beauty of green grass and wild flowers adorning our roots?"

With as much excitement as the birch could muster, he said, "What joy and delight when we awake from our deep sleep and begin to be dressed by God with buds and beautiful green leaves, as life springs into our branches."

And the elm rocked slowly in the breeze and said, "And how proud we are to see that you have survived the winter!"

The evergreen giggled, "So you do notice our beauty and steadfastness. How precious of you!"

The oak grunted and fell asleep.

Well, you only need to watch and listen to nature to reaffirm that there is a time and a season for all things. You can imagine what I shared with the group when we reassembled. The peace and comfort I was experiencing brought to mind that there is no dying in the Lord. We make a transition according to His mercy and grace, and wait patiently to see His face. I sat down on one of the park benches and read Psalm 84.

"How lovely is thy dwelling place,
O Lord Almighty!
My soul yearns, even faints for the courts
of the Lord; my heart and my flesh cry out
For the living God.

Even the sparrow has found a home, and
The swallow a nest for herself, where
she may have her young –
A place near your altar,
O Lord Almighty, my King and
my God.
Blessed are those who dwell in your
house;

I know now that in the midst of the turmoil of life, there is perfect peace and serenity in meditating on God's greatness. He made the world and all there is in it. And He made it all for us. We must learn to enjoy His presence, to trust His power, and teach others how to experience this perfect peace.

PSALM 98

A Meditation for the Theme of Unity

"O sing unto the Lord a new song; For He hath done marvelous things".

This Psalm calls for us to celebrate God's saving grace in song. It is a call to all the people worshipping in the temple and the congregation. It is a call to all people of the earth and a call to the whole creation, even the mountains and the seas, and all created things, to worship Him in song.

> *"The Lord has made known His salvation: His righteousness hath He openly shewed in the sight of the heathen."*

This is evidence that music is important to God. Throughout the Old Testament there were prophetic calls to worship God and to announce and exalt the coming of the Messiah – a way made for the salvation of His people. Therefore, these songs were joyous and full of praise.

Isaiah 9:6 says: For unto us a child is born, unto us a son is given; and the government shall be upon His shoulder, and His name shall be called Wonderful, Counselor, The Mighty God, the Everlasting Father, The Prince of Peace.

Just how important is music to God? Many of the answers are found in the Book of Psalms. There are songs that teach, that celebrate and worship the coming of Christ. There are songs that tell of God's goodness and power, and songs that show God's love for us. There are many songs for the confession of sin and the expression of sorrow. There are also songs that teach us to pray and trust God, and how to worship in His presence.

God created angels to worship Himself. They were with Him before He formed the earth. And throughout the Bible we find them leading heavenly host in singing praises to God.

According to the Greek interpretation and paralleling Isaiah 14:11-15, Lucifer was the lead angel. Not only was he the lead, but God had implanted the musical instruments in his body so that he would accompany the singing of heavenly host. He was beautiful. He was referred to as *The morning Star.* But in all his splendor, he became arrogant and tried to exalt himself above God. He was cast out of heaven and thrown down to earth. He is now Satan, or the devil, who tempted Adam and Eve, but could not tempt Jesus into worshiping him. Needless-to-say, he is still trying to get people to worship him, even through his music. Can't you hear it? And we must be careful that we do not imitate the corruption suggested in his music. Instead of holy and righteous expressions, we could be sending the wrong message to the world. God wants us to be alert and clear in our worship and praise of Him alone. Therefore, we must *"Make a joyful noise unto the Lord".*

Music has always been important in war. The armed men followed the priest who marched around the city of Jericho blowing the trumpets and rams' horns. Upon God's command to Joshua, the people shouted and the walls of Jericho came tumbling down. Joshua's only weapon was music. Read about it in the sixth chapter of Joshua.

There is healing power in music. Music has the power to set our minds and spirits free. Hospitals are using music therapy for soothing and relaxing patients. There are records showing amnesia being successfully treated with the aid of music. When King Saul who had an evil spirit at times became sick and depressed, he sent for David to play on his harp and, after a time, he was ready to perform his kingly duties again. Read 1st Samuel, chapter 16.

Music in the church should lead to restoration and revival; the strengthening of faith that once was, or reviving those who are dead to Christ. Music sets the stage for the Holy Spirit to come in and do His work. In order to do this, the ministry of song must first be filled with the Holy Spirit. Zachariah 4:6 says, "Not by might, not by power, but by my Spirit, saith the Lord".

We have an awesome task before us. It is important that musicians and singers be anointed by the Holy Spirit when we come before the people. If we are together, on one accord, lifting up our voices with one sound to worship and praise the Lord, there is unity.

We receive this anointing through studying scripture and sincere prayer which will bring unity into the Spirit. Without prayer, there will be no unity and harmony that will please God, and very often it will not please the spirit of the people. Our singing will be just mere words. We cannot adequately minister to the congregation unless the Spirit of God guides us.

Psalm 95: O come let us sing unto the Lord, let us make a joyful noise to the rock of our salvation. Let us come before his presence with thanksgiving, and make a joyful noise unto Him with psalms. Verse 6: O come, let us worship and bow down; let us kneel before the Lord our maker.

Unity of the Spirit opens the door to praise and worship. We play an important part in the worship service. We lay the groundwork for the total worship experience. We sing a song which indicates that if we don't praise Him, the rocks will take our place. There is no wonder that verses 7 and 8 of Psalm 98 is a call to all creation to praise Him.

> *"Let the sea roar, and the fullness thereof; The world, and they that dwell therein. Let the floods clap their hands; Let the hills be joyful together ...*

In closing, one of the most exciting revelations for the redeemed music lovers is to learn that there will be music in Heaven. Revelations 6:11-12 says:

> *"And I heard the voice of many angels round about the throne ... saying with a loud voice, 'Worthy is the Lamb that was slain' ..."*

The Love of Jesus
Meditation

In the gospel of Mark, Jesus was challenged by a would-be critic about the first commandment, and He taught: "To love God with all your heart, mind, soul, and strength". Then He gave him the second greatest: "To love thy neighbor as thyself". We know that if we love our neighbor as ourselves, we will not kill, steal, covet, bear false witness, and so on. Loving God and loving our neighbor is Jesus' highest expectation of us. He defended this in Matthew 5:17: "Think not that I am come to destroy the law, or the prophets; I am not come to destroy the law, but to fulfill it".

The critic was not surprised, because first century Judaism knew that in the Old Testament, Leviticus and Deuteronomy had laid down the basis of the Law. Even in Exodus, Moses realized the depths of the love of the Lord. In the song he led the Israelites in singing in the 15th chapter of Exodus, his message was: "Who among the gods is like you, O Lord ... In your unfailing love you will lead the people you have redeemed".

Our neighbors are people all over the world; the rich, the poor, the downtrodden, the hungry, and those who have never met Jesus. Jesus knew our hearts would not have the capacity to feel the 'warm fuzzies' for people who seem to be so hard to love; the neighbor next door who insists on throwing garbage on the street; the co-worker who has a habit of cutting everybody up with a sharp tongue; the child who spitefully hurts his peers including your child, and many others. So He taught in Luke 6:27-31: "But I tell you who hear me; Love your enemies, do good to those who hate you, bless those who curse you, pray for those who mistreat you. If someone strikes you on one cheek, turn to him the other also. If someone takes your cloak, do not stop him from taking your tunic. Give to everyone who asks you, and if anyone takes what belongs to you, do not demand it back. Do to others as you would have them do to you."

Now some of us meet these kinds of situations every day. We are stressed to the limit and feel the need to <u>vent.</u> So what are we to do? Well, we have <u>not</u> been commanded to feel love, but to act sincerely in a loving manner. This is AGAPE love. This kind of love causes us to treat others in a considerate manner regardless of how we feel about them. John 4:20 says, "those who say they love God whom they have not seen and do not love their brother is a liar".

AGAPE love involves a decision of the will, not a feeling of the heart. So, is Jesus telling us to give up our rights to retaliate or to respond in kind? Absolutely. The key question is, will the cause of Christ suffer if we satisfy our own selfish emotions? People need to see Christianity demonstrated. Showing love is a Christian's trademark. AGAPE love requires that we (1) treat others with kindness and consideration; (2) put aside rudeness, meanness, and spite; (3) avoid exclusion and cliquish behavior; (4) reach out to those who might feel unloved and lost. It challenges us to demonstrate to the world, our neighbors, what Christianity is all about. It is more than feelings of "warm fuzzies"; more than kindness and consideration. Love is ultimately a willingness to help someone else no matter what the cost, and to do it unconditionally. Jesus taught this at the Last Supper in John 15:13: "Greater love hath no man than this, that a man lay down his life for his friends". Jesus did it for us on the cross. What are we doing to show that we are His friend and friends of our neighbors?

Perfect Peace

Meditation

I have pity for the man who goes through life and can't seem to find peace. He stumbles along a path of no return.
He catches the dust of every passing wind, but never stops to watch the leaves race quickly and safely to earth!

On an early spring morning, has he heard the sweet and cheerful sound of a bird outside his window, high up in a tree, singing a wake-up song?

And has he watched the sunrise on a summer morn and gazed at the magnificent goldenrod upon the hillside, or seen the bright green leaves of corn breaking through the rich brown earth, and watched them slowly rise to harvest?

And where is he when the quiet breezes pass through the trees at eventide when the noises of day are diminishing; and did he pause to hear the crickets sing their songs of the night as the hours pass to midnight and on to dawn?

Did he ever watch a baby sleeping in her crib – the slight rhythmic movement of her breathing, and the smile on the mother's face as she slowly tiptoes away, and falls asleep upon her pillow?

Was there ever a time when he sat quietly and meditated on the love of God; how God, without warning moved a stumbling block our of his way? When was it God caused him to move quickly out of harm's way? Does he remember when God showed His love through a friend or a stranger's concern? And has he paused to count how much God provided when times were tough?

I suggest that he find a grassy spot, lie flat on his back and watch the patches of cloud move slowly across the clear blue sky, and try to make sense of the shapes as they slide along; and finally, close his eyes and see the awesome face of God.

This is Perfect Peace!

Ephesus

A brief study of one of the seven churches from the Book of Revelations, Chapter One

Amphitheater at Ephesus
pictured in the "Encyclopedia Of The Bible"

ENCYCLOPEDIA OF THE BIBLE, by Walter A. Elwell, Baker Book House, Grand Rapids, Michigan. Page 129.

EPHESUS

A Brief History of
A Wealthy City in Asia Minor

Ephesus was an ancient city founded by Greek Colonists in early 1000 b.c. It was known for its many religions including Emporer worship, occult practices, Hellenized Judaism, and early Christianity.

The city was located on an inland harbor, connected to the Cayster River by a narrow channel which flowed into the Aegean Sea.

Because of its location, Ephesus was the most important city on the western shore of Asia Minor, and quickly became a major commercial center and a means of travel to and from other eastern provinces. It soon became the Capital of the Roman province of Asia.

Ephesus was an emporium - a sort of melting pot that had few equals anywhere in the world in terms of population and natural resources. It ranked with Rome, Corinth, Antioch and Alexandria.

Wealth was flowing in the city of marble streets and civic monuments. Ephesus boasted of its marble streets lined with a shopping center (agora), a marble fountain, library, baths and beautiful houses. Some of the homes for the upper-middle class had mosaic floors and marble walls. Also, scattered among them were gambling houses and houses of prostitution.

Ephesus was a major trade route, and so the merchants were a constant but transient part of the population, as well as tourists who frequented theTemple of Artemis, known to the Romans as "Diana".

The Temple built in the early 6th century b.c. was the largest edifice in the Hellenistic world. It was constructed entirely of marble and was considered one of the seven wonders of the ancient world. Silversmiths made a fortune crafting shrines and images of the multi-breasted Goddess, Diana. Paul almost lost his life there preaching against idols. Because his preaching affected the sales of these statues, the people started rioting in an effort to silence Paul for good. Acts 19:23-41.

Paul realized how difficult it was for the Christians there to live out the gospel in such a challenging place. So he spent more time in establishing and nurturing the church there than with any of the other churches.

Ephesus had been a city about a thousand years before Paul made his third missionary journey. His travel mission to the seven churches was easier because the cities were located approximately 100 miles apart, connected by a great triangular highway.

Paul preached in the Grand Theater mentioned in Acts 19:29. It was built in three tiers, and is known to have seated 24,000 people.

The impact of Christianity was felt in Ephesus and other churches in the region for centuries. The 3rd Ecumenical Council was held in 431 A.D. in the Church of Mary. This council established Mary's place as "The Mother of God" in Western Catholic Theology.

Commerce began to decline after the harbor silted up, and looting by the Goths began. The harbor became 20 miles of reeds and marshland, and the ships left. There was an attempt to reconstruct, but the job was too great. Ephesus, early in the 1st century was a dying city.

Persecution by the Romans was taking its toll. The Persians moved in and the war began. Most of the apostles had been killed, along with hundreds of thousands Christians under Emperors Domitian and Trajan.

After Paul's death, John tried to revive the churches until he was exiled on Patmos. So, what has happened in that region? If you will check a map of Turkey, you will find that it is a large country that lies between the Mediterranean and the Black seas. It is about the size of Texas, and extends into southern Europe and covers the Peninsula of Asia Minor where the churches were located.

But the history of strife and wars for control of the region had been going on since approximately 1500 b.c. The first historic rulers of the province were the Hittites. And the wars continued. Many small kingdoms rose and fell in that period before 63 b.c.

Then the Romans under Pompey conquered the area and ruled for hundreds years. They brought some peace to the region with the exception of religious strife. Roman rule was emperor worship, and Christians were persecuted.

When the Turks moved in, they brought with them a strong love for the country and the people. Approximately 98% of the people were Moslems, and freedom of worship was permitted. They took control of the government and adopted a Western way of life. They seemed to prosper in all areas except in education. At the end of WW1, only 8 persons out of 10 could read and write.

In 1925, there was tension between Russia and Turkey over the waterways, the Bosporus and the Dardenelles. This continued until 1947 when President Truman signed the Truman Doctrine giving aid to countries threatened by outside forces. Turkey received millions of dollars and in turn, the United States set up a military base there. You know the pattern ... you help somebody, and you are in!

Finally, maps for this study were found in the New International Version Study Bible. The following places were located on the map of Turkey found in The World Book Encyclopedia:

1. The Isle of Patmos where John was a prisoner
2. Izmir – city of Smyrna
3. Ephesus – city was uncovered by archeologists in the 1800s.
4. Philadelphia – now Alesehir
5. Ankara – the capital city was formerly Galatia
6. Tarsus, where Paul was born
7. Antioch, where apostles were first called Christians. Paul visited Lydia there and they held church by the river.

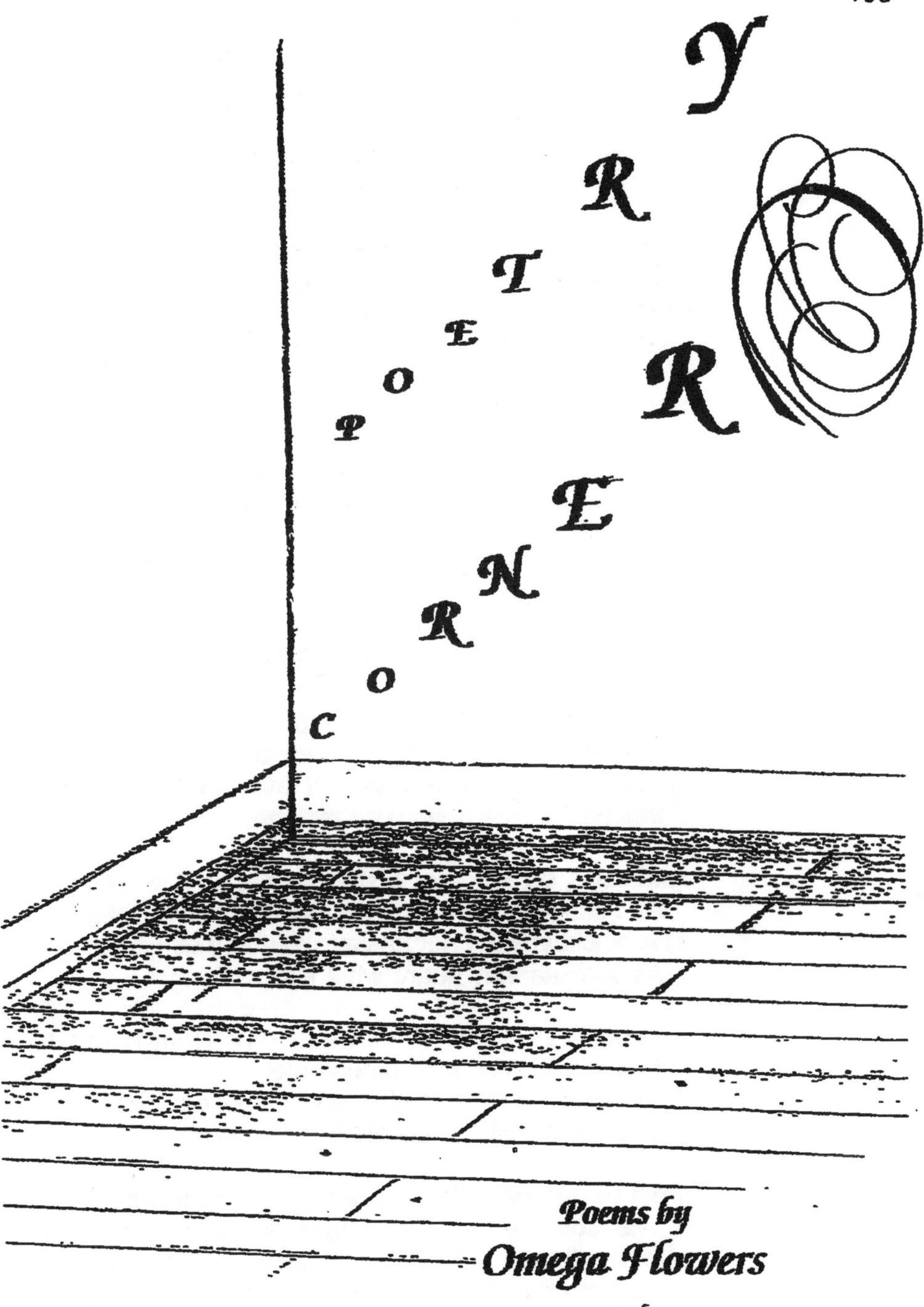

Poems by

Omega Flowers

and

Sabrina Flowers Rogers

A Choir is Born

All was quiet one morning in spring,
'Til one bird decided to sing!
The sparrows went hopping from branch to branch
And the wrens went scattering on wings.

Then there was some flitting and chasing about
That sounded like a broken oboe.
But if truth were known, they were jealous
Of each other's imposing crescendo.

Now look who stood up and observed it all;
The ostrich with great disappointment!
How can a whole species that loved to chatter
Act in such a brash manner?

The wren, a soprano, just gossiped in high C;
The blackbird, an alto, just chuckled;
The robin, whose voice was a beautiful tenor,
Traded chides with the hoot owl's basso.

So the ostrich started gently flapping his wings,
And attention, you bet he commanded,
'Til all were quieted and started swaying
In time with the rhythm he planted.

And soon, oh, so quietly, sparrows started singing.
And bluejays joined the rhythm that was brewing;
The blackbirds did not hesitate to add their vibrato
As soon as they heard what was stewing.

The hoot owls listened, they turned and they listened,
To the beautiful, melodious tune;
And they moaned and grunted 'til all of a sudden
They bounced in staccato and crooned.

That ostrich was beaming, and swaying, and beaming
The movement was soaring on wings.
What a glorious sound was heard near and far.
On the wings of that morning in spring.

Which Gate, Matthew?

Matthew 7:13

Let's explore the passage, "the way to God's Kingdom", I said to my friend one Saturday evening.

He thought I meant the infamous north side caves
where robbers and thieves hid their loot and the
slaves, they kept to do their jobs on the shady side.
He was ready for an exciting, but horrible ride
through dangers seen and unseen, you see.
I believe he would have joined them if it weren't
for me. He said, "I like to stretch my legs, you see,
And I think the wide gate is better for me.
Besides, the narrow gate is too hard to find;
You can search and search 'til you're out of
your mind, and no time is left to hang out with
your friends who will cover your back to the bitter
end. That's what I like," he said.

So I sat him down and told him a story;
How Jesus gave his life for us and went on to Glory
to sit at the right hand of God and do our bidding.
He looked at me as if I were kidding.
But I continued, "If we give our hearts and minds
over for directions, we can count on God's love and
His protection. What His son did for us proves He is
our Savior, For who else would go to the cross in our
stead; or even give us our daily bread?

So we don't have to guess which gate to enter.
The one that leads to God's kingdom is strait.
And many have gone down the wrong way already,
and few have found the narrow gate".
He said, "That's the gate for me".

Cheer Up!

Come, my love!
Just let me hold your aching head.
You're much too young to be grieving
'Tis a pity your heart weighs of lead.

Why not hold up your head and face it.
Must you grieve o'er what's past and gone?
The world waits to rejoice with you
Don't cry, or you'll cry alone.

There are hundreds of goals out there for you
Choose wisely and make a new start
For the world needs men of your ability
And remember, you still have my heart.

Love Letters

In my pocket there's a letter
Resting gently near my heart
It's a testimony of dear friendship
Total proof its words impart.

The contents are born of kindness
Pleasure lurks in every line
Faith reaches out beyond measure
Swells my heart with hope divine.

And my mind no longer wonders
If your heart belongs to me
For I trust in you completely
Fate will take our course, you see.

One day far out on the ocean
You'll come sailing back to me
'Til then, Darling, I am with you
And with me you'll always be.

The Storm

One day the clouds came from the south
And passed beneath the sun,
They ceased their movement with the wind
And stayed until the dawn.

As hours passed, the earth darkened
And rain came quietly down,
Thunder rumbled to break the quietness,
And streets emptied all over town.

And soon the wind was howling
And rattling the window panes,
The lightning streaked across the sky
As the storm roared on like trains.

After hours, the quietness came back,
Like a thief, it tiptoed in
Filling each corner with an eerie hush!
You could hear the drop of a pin.

We dared to peek through the shutters
Hoping lightning would not blast our eyes,
But streets were clean and trees were still
We could go again outside!

If It Is Not Enough

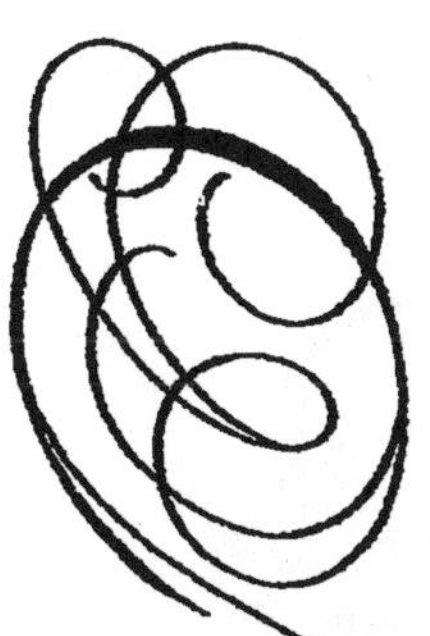

God grant us peace in our souls
And we'll encourage peace.
If all we do is not enough
You speak and wars will cease.

Lord grant us grace to run the race
This life of ups and downs
If all we do is not enough
Your love always abounds.

Christmas Mystery

Now Christmas is coming, you girls and boys
Have you started thinking of goodies and toys?
Are you planning to stay up to see Santa this year?
To watch him ride in on his sleigh pulled by reindeer?

Oh! What's this already – a little bundle of red?
Is it a doll? I saw it earlier on the bed;
And it moved last night, but I don't know where,
Maybe it's hidden and waiting just under the stair.

Whatever it is, it seems alive, I know.
For I saw it moving close to the door.

Oh, look! Now it's moving towards the Christmas tree
It slides on its stomach instead of the knee.

No, wait! I believe I can see its head,
Oops! There it goes again under the bed.
Let's wait and watch as it makes its exit;
Oh, look! There it is, it's little Alexis!

It's not a red truck, or a doll, or a toy.
It's little Alexis, that bundle of joy!

My Mother's Love

Thanks be to God for blessing me
With precious gifts from above
The most wondrous of all, I know you'll agree
Is the gift of my mother's love.

With God's help, she built a strong foundation
That would withstand any trial or test
She taught me the value of education
Paving the road for my future success.

Even today, my mother's example teaches me
Lessons that will guide my life 'til the end
My strength and courage come from her, you see
She's more than my mom; she's my best friend.

And now, as we approach my wedding day
I'm reminded of times shared together
As always, she's only a phone call away
I'll love you, Ma, always and forever!

Sabrina
July 29, 2000

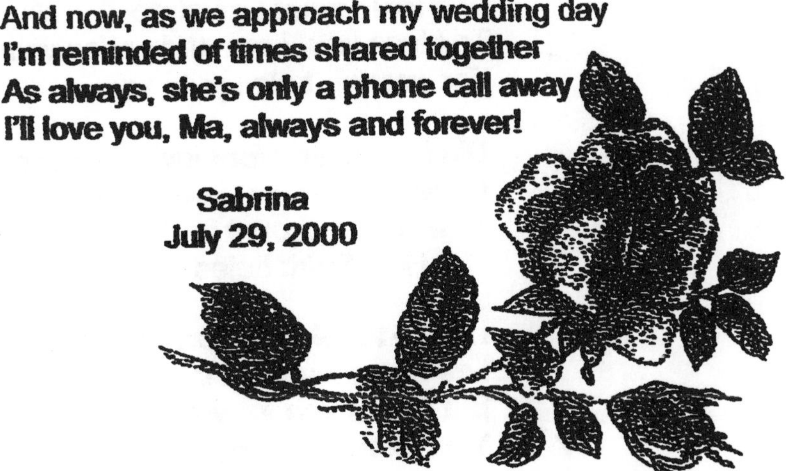

Did I Forget?

Did I forget to thank you, Lord
When my eyes saw the light of day?
Or did I find night's deep darkness
Standing boldly in my way?

Did I forget to thank you, Lord
For the morsel of food I ate?
For my body needed nourishment
Before it was too late.

Did I forget to read Your Word
And learn what I must do
To bless you, Lord and praise your name?
For worship belongs to you.

Did I thank you for amazing grace;
Blessings I could never earn?
How can I account for the spiritual growth
The Holy Spirit helps me to learn?

Let me thank you now for your precious care
I ask for no special favors;
But praise you for your wonderful gift,
Your Son, my wonderful Saviour.

And So, I Write ...

by Omega Flowers

ISBN: 0-2761600-1-5

For your convenience in ordering additional copies of this book, use one of the two methods:

1. Contact your local bookstore and give the ISBN number
2. Complete the form below for postal orders:

Name:____

Address:____________________City________________

State:______________________Zip code______________

Telephone:______________________________________

E-mail:____

Price: $19.95 (add $3.00 for shipping and handling. If you order two books or more, include an additional $1.50 for shipping and handling; i.e. 2 books, $4.50, etc.)

Number of books:____
Total amount enclosed: _______________(check or money order)

\-

M

Mantel Publishing
P.O. Box 361281
Decatur, GA. 30034
Phone: (770) 322-8403
E-mail: flores999@aol.com